BEGINNINGS
BUT NO ENDING

BEGINNINGS
BUT NO ENDING

An Autobiography

by
Nevile Davidson

THE EDINA PRESS
EDINBURGH

THE EDINA PRESS LTD
1 ALBYN PLACE, EDINBURGH EH2 4NG

First published 1978

ISBN O 905695 07 0

Printed in Scotland by
Office Printing Services
21 Stafford Street, Edinburgh EH3 7BJ

Contents

Foreword

At his death, Dr Nevile Davidson left behind him a recently completed autobiography. It is now published in abbreviated form. Nothing of substance has been omitted and the wording is his own throughout.

His father, born into a Free Church home, in 1853, belonged to that generation of Scottish ministers who, without changing the substance of their faith, passed from a Calvinist upbringing into a more liberal way. Similarly, as he tells here, Dr Davidson's own outlook changed. As a young man he read with understanding and sympathy theologians till then little known in Scotland; but he was always more concerned with the practice of the Christian life than with its theory and it was in the conduct of worship that the change was seen. He did not choose the coldness and occasional bleakness so often found in the worship of an older Scotland, but was not without respect for its austerity; on the other hand, his time as an assistant minister left him with a mild distaste for the concept of the popular preacher and a stronger one for rhetorical prayers addressed more to the congregation than to God. As any reader will see, his love and respect for his father were very deep, but an alternative title for his life story might have been, "Between Two Worlds."

This is equally true of the other side of his family background. His mother came from one of the older landed families of Scotland and this gave him family contacts which are far from common in the Scottish ministry. Glasgow is an industrial city and the Townhead, where the Cathedral stands, was not merely the oldest quarter of the city but also its poorest and most decayed. In recent years the worst of the slums have been demolished, but it was not so in his time. He does not tell of the long hours which he spent, very happily, visiting in these surroundings. Far more of his care and attention was given to the least privileged members of his congregation than to the more prosperous.

A great deal is left untold in these pages. He was not one to tell of the devotion and prayer that filled his life, for despite the dignity he always showed, he was a man of modesty and humility. His assistants were told that they should prepare their sermons carefully but never read them. Prayers were to be read. As far as possible they were to be in words of one syllable and, if an Anglo-Saxon word was available, it should be preferred to one derived from the Latin. Simplicity was part of the reverence due to God. Though he loved the measured prose of Cranmer, late in his life he began to say "You" in prayer instead of "Thou".

In the same way he tells nothing of the quiet courage which he always showed. It was said that in his boyhood he used to cycle along the top of a wall. Asked if it was true he replied, "Yes. There was no problem in it. The only problem was to get off!" In those North Berwick days he was known as Nevile the devil. When he came to Glasgow the task before him was a terrifying one; as the city centre decayed the membership moved further and further out into the more distant suburbs. In addition, as the minister of Glasgow, it was necessary to maintain contact with every aspect of the public life of the city. Younger members of Cathedral families naturally joined local churches, and the burden of pastoral care and public activities might have dismayed many men. As for the condition of the great building, the present writer vividly remembers its atmosphere of Victorian gloom when he visited it for the first time in 1927; a hand laid on Archbishop Law's tomb left a visible imprint in the deposit of grime.

No one should accept at face value his confessions of idleness. He had an orderly mind and orderly habits, and a great capacity for work. His records of the family life and interests of his members were meticulous. It was his custom to arrive in the vestry half an hour before worship so that there would be no haste or excitement, to leave for prayer with the choir at five minutes before the service, and to enter the church exactly on the minute. A leisurely manner concealed the amount of work he accomplished. He never seemed to be in a hurry. When people came to see him at awkward moments he had the gift of giving them the assurance that he had listened to them at length and dealt with their problem and yet of getting rid of them quickly. In private he had a great sense of humour which, otherwise, could sometimes only be seen in his eyes and the slight smile. And his courtesy was unfailing. The writer was present when a man of notorious ill nature was grossly rude to him; neither at the time nor afterwards did he show any sign of resentment. He never seemed impatient or angry.

On 20 December 1977 he had called at a house in Edinburgh and returned to his car to drive away. A passing policemen found him seated at the wheel, but there was no answer. Only those who lived and worked with him will know how kind and good he was.

James Bulloch

1

Home and University

For the great majority of people physical surroundings have a strong influence on development and character. The manse of my childhood stood close to the shore of the Firth of Forth. Across a small expanse of garden and a narrow road we looked out to a sandy bay. At high tide the sound of the waves drifted in at our windows; in times of mist the foghorn sounded; and after dark the beams from the lighthouses on the Bass Rock and the May shone across the water. To grow up within sight and sound of the sea is to acquire a sense of the majesty and mystery of the universe. My earliest recollections are of the daily walks along the shore with my sister and our young German nurse, the yellow sands and rock pools full of crabs and sea anemones. This was a formidable rocky coast and almost every winter ships were wrecked. More than once, even in summer time, we saw a swimmer drowned in our bay and his body carrried ashore. As far back as I can remember one of the chief influences in my life was the wonder of the natural world.

The other chief influence was the atmosphere of home. My father came of farming stock in Buchan, a countryside breeding men of strong and independent character. As his father had died young the family moved to Aberdeen, and there he graduated Master of Arts at King's College. He never spoke much of these years except to say that in their home there was the utmost simplicity and that money was never plentiful. Financial stringency made it necessary for him to spend two years teaching in a country school; but the difficulties were overcome and a few years later he graduated as Bachelor of Divinity at the University of Edinburgh. Education was valued, and many a student and his family were ready to make sacrifices for it. I think the quietly accepted austerity of those early days, combined with the high moral and religious ideals of his home life, were influences which never left him. Even as children we were subconsciously aware of it. We used to mock affectionately at the large bowl of porridge which was his invariable breakfast, and at his enjoyment of plain rice pudding or rhubarb jam or potato soup. He never smoked, and was a life long total abstainer. He spent little on clothes, dressing at all times in a clerical suit of strong black tweed. His only extravagance was books; and his upstairs study, looking out to the sea, contained a splendid library, displaying an astonishingly wide outlook and catholicity of interest.

1

My sister and I as we grew up could not fail to notice that our father was a man of completely dedicated and completely disciplined life. He had felt a call to the ministry and obedience to that call was the dominating force in all his after life. Ordained and inducted to the charge of the Blackadder Church in North Berwick, he remained there for the whole course of his ministry, resisting many approaches and invitations to move to larger or more lucrative spheres. His days were carefully regulated and planned. Except for Mondays, the morning was always spent in reading, writing, and sermon preparation. In the afternoon he visited ill and old parishioners. Two evenings in the week were kept for regular pastoral visitation. On Saturday afternoons almost invariably he walked to the top of the Law with its far stretching views.

My father was a devoted pastor, knowing with individual interest and affection all those committed to his spiritual care, respected by almost everyone in the small town. He treated all alike with the same natural and old fashioned courtesy, although perhaps his chief concerns were the poor and the humble. As a preacher he was theological and biblical, but almost always with a message relevant to everyday life. His sermons were carefully prepared and meticulously written out. Often, going into his study unexpectedly, one would find him on his knees with an open Bible; and at least in later years, one would realise the source of his personal faith and his spiritual influence in the community. I have attempted to write this pen portrait of my father because, looking back, I realise how strong and deep was the effect in our home, not so much in words as in the silent example of Christian character at its finest.

My mother came from a very different social background. Her father, Sir Andrew Agnew, was the eighth baronet; the family had lived in Wigtownshire for some six hundred years and for more than three hundred had been Hereditary Sheriffs of Galloway. In the home where she spent her first thirty years, Lochnaw Castle, she had known every comfort and the utmost security. She herself was deeply religious. She had been confirmed into the Church of England but always when at home attended the parish church of Leswalt. My father and she shared the same strong beliefs and she gave him wholehearted support in his ministry.

As I grew up the household included a cook, a young housemaid, an elderly laundry maid, and my sister's governess. The day began with family prayers in the study. My mother played a small harmonium for a psalm or hymn. After a short reading from the Bible we knelt for prayers. My father had a wonderful gift of prayer, and apart from the words his reverence left an impression of the reality of communion with God which has gone with me through all the years.

My mother was quick, determined, and autocratic, never hesitating to rebuke or express disapproval. She was punctilious in details and would have had small respect for permissiveness. Respect for older people and those in authority were regarded as axiomatic. For us children, her word was law. But in my mother, discipline was accompanied by intense affection. She loved to have us with her. Every evening after tea, on the long winter evenings, she would read aloud to us. Always she would come to say goodnight to us in bed. Often we had punishment, but as soon as it was over the bad deed was forgotten. She never doubted either her own authority or her wisdom of judgement. When, some years later, she knew that she was dying, her one passionate regret was that she had to leave us bereft of her loving care.

Owing to periodic bouts of asthma and bronchitis I was not sent to school at the usual age and my early education was given by my parents, but at ten I was sent to the High School at North Berwick. It was not at that time a very large school, with something like a hundred pupils, and it was, of course, coeducational. Neither lessons nor examinations gave me any anxiety, but I was incurably and unrepentantly lazy, and though I never failed in any examinations I had no desire to earn any distinction and hardly ever gained any prizes. We had an excellent headmaster, Mr Thomas Glover, a man of irascible temper but of the highest ideals. As the years passed I gradually discovered that I intensely disliked chemistry and mildly disliked mathematics. The learning of French was worthwhile since it was a charmingly elegant language. But the subject which, far beyond all others, appealed to me was English literature. Palgrave's *Golden Treasury* became the door into a new world.

In winter months in addition to the Sunday services my father had a prayer meeting on Wednesdays and a service for children on Fridays, often enlivened by lantern slides. Once a year he visited every household in the congregation, announcing on Sunday in which part of the town he would be. Almost invariably he read some verses from a pocket New Testament and always said a prayer. Sometimes I was with him and was struck by the naturalness with which he did this and the appreciation it received. My mother's special interest was the cause of Foreign Missions, for which she organised a Sale of Work every year.

During summer months the atmosphere was very different. North Berwick attracted thousands of people, so that there seemed to be a constant stream of visitors. It was a very cosmopolitan stratum of society, made up of people of different background and outlook. Conversation was correspondingly varied. Even my father could sometimes be roused to heated political argument. In the next terrace Sir Auckland and Sir Eric Geddes always spent some weeks and my father and they usually found themselves in agreement. Others were rigidly Conservative. One, whom we knew as Cousin Agnita, as she entered the house would throw out some taunt such as, "Do you see that terrible man, Lloyd George, is now proposing his impossible insurance schemes and pensions?'', well knowing that my father, a staunch Liberal, would not be able to resist a furious verbal conflict. Many of our friends were members of the Church of England. Those of the Evangelical tradition felt at home in our presbyterian forms of worship and I remember when old Prebendary Webb-Peploe of St Paul's Cathedral gave a Bible exposition in our church.

Our family holidays took place in late spring or early autumn, but we also went on short visits to relations. One of the nearest was Humbie House, the home of the Master of Polwarth whose wife was a cousin of my mother. Cousin Walter, as we called him, always read family prayers in the dining room just before breakfast in a stentorian tone of voice, since his wife was deaf. Only gradually did we realise that he was one of the kindest of men. He was Chief Commissioner of Prisons for Scotland, Convener of the County of East Lothian, and a devoted elder of the parish church. By far the most exciting visits were to Rossie Priory, the Perthshire home of one of my mother's sisters who had married Lord Kinnaird. On arrival at the station we were met by a carriage drawn by two strong black horses, accompanied by a coachman and footman. I was allowed to sit on the box and now and again take the reins. It was at Rossie Priory that my father and mother had first met and from the Kinnairds' London house in St James's Square they were later married in St James's Church, Piccadilly.

Twice we had spent an annual holiday at Nethy Bridge, and in 1910 my parents decided to build a house there. All the land in that part belonged to the Seafield family and the old Countess was rather reluctant to permit new building. However, my father was allowed to take a feu of about two acres on the edge of the forest. Completely secluded, the house had three sitting rooms and eight bedrooms and so allowed us to have many friends and relations to stay. For the next sixty years it was to be my second home.

In 1914 all suddenly changed. August 4th was a beautiful summer's morning. We had just finished family prayers when we heard a voice calling my father by name. It was my cousin, Kenneth Kinnaird, returning from bathing: ''James, I hear that war has been declared!'' Only a short time afterwards Kenneth left home to join The Scottish Horse. The first years of the War did not greatly affect the pattern of life of those who belonged to the younger generation. School life had to go on as usual. A battalion of the Royal Scots were quartered in the town. Many were given hospitality in private houses, including our manse. And still the war dragged on and on.

At sixteen I passed my Higher Leaving Certificate examination, which meant exemption from a university entrance examination. I was very immature in many ways, very shy, very sparsely educated. But there was a restlessness in the air. Another year or two at school would have been of value but I was tired of school and foolishly persuaded my parents that there was no point in staying on any longer. It was therefore decided that I should matriculate at Edinburgh University in October, still living at home and travelling to Edinburgh each day. This arrangement was regrettable. It meant that I took little part in the wider life of the university and simply attended classes. The subjects I had chosen were Latin, History and English. The professor of History was a distinguished teacher, Sir Richard Lodge, who had no warmth of personality. Apparently arrogant and aloof, he seldom recognised any of his students even when meeting them in the quadrangle; but he commanded respect if not affection. But the subject which appealed to me above all was English Literature.

As the war proceeded slowly and heavily on my father, though now past sixty, offered his services to the Y.M.C.A. and went out to Dieppe for a long spell of duty. I had joined the Officers' Training Corps and become a member of the artillery battery. The university session finished, and the time came when I could apply for a commission in the Royal Artillery. I was sent to a Cadet School near Freshwater in the Isle of Wight. Among the cadets were many of my own age, but also older men promoted from the ranks, and for me it was a very new kind of experience. In due course I received my commission and was posted for further training, but by now the war had drawn to an end. After the first exhilaration had begun to fade it was succeeded by a sense of lethargy and discontent. The chief desire of most was to be set free to return to familiar ways.

I was not demobilised until January 1919; and although the winter session was half over I decided to resume my studies at the University. I had cherished the hope of an honours course in English Literature, but changed my mind and decided to read for a degree in Mental Philosophy.

Professor Andrew Pringle Pattison was about to retire from the Chair of Logic and Metaphysics and I had the privilege of attending some of his last lectures. He was succeeded by one who quickly became and for ever after remained one of the most intellectually stimulating and personally noble men I have known, Professor Norman Kemp Smith. A native of Dundee and a graduate of St Andrews, he had for some ten years occupied the Chair of Psychology at Princeton. The war made him anxious to return to Britain. Being ineligible for military service because of his age he held a post in the Department of Information of the War Office and the Admiralty, and later in the American section of the Ministry of Information. In June 1919 he was elected to the Edinburgh Chair and on 10 October delivered his inaugural lecture, "The Present Situation in Philosophy."

Many years afterwards, one of his students wrote, "One recalls the crowded class room of nearly 300 students, most of them ex-service men, restless and expectant, ready to show their impatience of teaching which seemed to be merely a carry-over from pre-war days: then the realization, when Kemp Smith began to speak, that they were in the presence of a supremely great teacher and a personality of commanding force.'' The other with whom I had much to do was Professor James Seth of the Chair of Moral Philosophy. Charming, quiet, and shy, he took an almost fatherly interest in his students. He was an excellent lecturer and a convinced Christian who won the respect and affection of all who came to know him.

This took me into a field of study concerned not with facts, but with thoughts, ideas, and speculations; the place of man in the universe, the existence of God, the possibility of immortality, different kinds of reasoning and of knowledge. During the first weeks under Kemp Smith I felt bewildered, but before long one felt a kind of intellectual excitement. As one moved into the honours classes the whole setting was different. The professor was no longer a distant potentate on a rostrum but a senior friend. As we sat round a table discussing Kant, Hume, Aristotle, or Spinoza we realised that we were being introduced to some of the greatest of thinkers.

But in 1920 this peaceful existence was darkened by the first great sorrow in my home life. Our mother began to show signs of illness. Increasingly in pain, she had to spend much of her day in bed. She and I had always been very close to each other. She intensely loved her husband, her children, and her home. Now she and we gradually became aware that she would have to leave us. Week by week, whenever I could escape from Edinburgh, I would sit for hours reading to her. On 20 June 1920 she slowly became unconscious, and then slept away, passing into the nearer presence of the God whom she had so completely trusted and tried to serve. We laid my mother's body to rest in the old churchyard of Abernethy. The influence of a truly good mother, her love, her prayers, her example go with one through all the years. My mother's memory has been one of the shaping and comforting influences of my whole life.

It was not easy to settle in to ordinary familiar patterns of life. With the beginning of the winter session in October I returned to Edinburgh and to the pleasant rooms in Strathearn Road which I had occupied for some three years. My landlady, old Mrs Charleson, old-fashioned and dignified, almost always dressed in the afternoons and evenings in a dress of black satin with a high collar. As she moved, it rustled smoothly. Her daughter lit the fire, made the beds, and laid the table, but Mrs Charleson herself always did any necessary conversation. I had an ordinary breakfast and invariably lunched out, usually at the Union, but the main meal was high tea at about 5.30 or 6 o'clock. I soon discovered not to expect much variety, but three dishes superlatively cooked; braised hotpot, grilled steak, or bacon and eggs. For the five days I paid her thirty shillings a week for my sitting room and bedroom, and for whatever food I had to eat. Often friends would sit talking until the small hours, but she never complained, a model landlady indeed.

I greatly enjoyed the work of another winter since it involved attendance at the small honours classes in Metaphysics and Moral Philosophy. A great deal of private reading was expected, and many books prescribed. In the early spring I entered for the Rhind scholarship, but only took second place. On re-opening my diary of that time I realise that my besetting sin of idleness was still unconquered. Perhaps it was partly because I was completely lacking in academic ambition, and partly due to a lack of inner self discipline. The result was that even as the final examinations drew near the seriousness of my own studies did not increase. When the results were announced I had only achieved second class honours. When I told my father the news he made no comment, but walked out of the room and scarcely spoke to me for the next few days. A slight consolation was that I was awarded a Vans Dunlop scholarship, and was offered the post of assistant lecturer in the Department of Logic and Metaphysics. What so deeply distressed me was the bitter disappointment to my father. It was a severe shock. But, in spite of many weaknesses through the years since then, I think I did overcome the idleness of those earlier years — although often with a struggle.

The following winter was pleasant and leisurely. My post as assistant was only part-time and consisted very largely in the correction of class exercises and examinations and the judging of essays. In addition I attended classes in English history and took piano lessons from Marjorie Kennedy Fraser. All of which still left time for wide ranging if rather desultory reading. As an antidote to purely mental activity I also did some riding and had lessons in jumping and enjoyed many a gallop below Arthur's Seat in the King's Park.

As my years at the University came to an end I knew that an important decision would have to be made. Was it to be, as I knew my parents had hoped, the ordained ministry, or some other career? I believed then, as I still believe, that no man should enter upon the holy ministry without a sense of vocation. Without that, a ministry would be both arid and miserable and impossibly demanding. The question inevitably led to considerable soul searching. It also raised the query as to what constitutes a call and how one becomes aware of it. Some can trace the awareness of such a call to a particular moment or spiritual experience. For others, brought up in a Christian home and religious atmosphere, the sense of vocation to the ministry comes gradually and almost imperceptibly. It is impossible to record any specific date or happening. Perhaps, for me, the clearest indication was a negative one; I could not imagine myself in any other way of life. In the end I became convinced that, however unworthy, I was being led towards the study of divinity and prepared for the life of a minister of the Gospel.

How did I reach that point and what influences had been silently at work in bringing me to it? I think the answer is twofold; through certain persons and through certain books. My father, reserved Scotsman as he was, never spoke much about religion; but one knew without any possible doubt that it was his religious beliefs which shaped the whole pattern of his life. We, his children, knew that his duties and responsibilities as a minister would always take priority over everything else. We enjoyed seeing friends and had a succession of visitors; but behind it all, my father allowed nothing to interfere with his disciplined way of life; retiring to his study to write and read in the mornings, going out to his pastoral visiting in the afternoons, interviewing people, or discussing church affairs with his session clerk. One noticed too how people of all kinds valued his friendship and respected his judgement, and how he was surrounded with affection so that when he walked along the street everyone wanted to catch his eye and have a word of greeting from him. And Sunday after Sunday from the pulpit there sounded the note of strong evangelical conviction and in the prayers a marvellous co-mingling of intimacy and awe.

This, then, in living personal expression, was the image of the ordained ministry gradually and only half-consciously conveyed to me by my father through the years of boyhood and adolescence; and through that close and profound influence God was perhaps drawing me also towards ordination and all it involved. Another influence derived from the privilege of meeting in our manse distinguished missionaries from overseas such as Donald Fraser of Livingstonia and Dr Webster of Manchuria. Those missionaries, sitting talking so modestly and earnestly to my father, were able men, statesmanlike in outlook, compassionate in heart, who might have made a notable place for themselves in our own country. Even in the conversation and the faces of these dedicated servants of Christ one could feel something of the supernatural power and appeal of the ministry at its best. Almost without any definite or dramatic decision it became clear to me that I should move on to the study of Divinity.

On 13 September I sat the entrance examination for New College, Edinburgh, and shortly afterwards began to attend the prescribed classes. As I still held a Vans Dunlop scholarship and also earned a small sum from the Department of Philosophy I was now financially independent and no longer needed to look to my father for help. The staff at New College comprised the Principal, Dr Alexander Martin, who lectured on Apologetics and played a large part in the negotiations for Church Reunion; Dr H.R. Mackintosh, who taught Dogmatics; Dr A.C. Welch, Professor of Old Testament and Dr William Manson, Professor of New Testament; Professor Hugh Watt, who taught Church History; Professor J.Y. Simpson who lectured on the relations of Science and

Religion; and Dr Harry Miller, who taught Sociology and had oversight of the mission in the Pleasance, a very rough and poor part of the city. It was a happy and fairly close knit community, though varied in background, outlook, and temperament.

I was not enough of a scholar to feel the fascination of detailed textual criticism, but Dr Welch's lectures on the Old Testament prophets held the class spell bound. By far the most stimulating subject was theology as expounded by H.R. Mackintosh. To turn from philosophy to theology was to find oneself in a new and refreshing world of thought. The field of thought, for the philosopher, is dominated by reason, but in Christian theology a new concept appears, revelation, made supremely in a Person, Jesus Christ, and in the Scriptures which bear witness to Him. In reply to that we are called to make a response of faith. As Karl Barth has said, "Theology responds to the Word which God has spoken, still speaks, and will speak again in the history of Jesus Christ." To pass from philosophy to theology is to pass from a realm of speculation to one of conviction.

Apart from classes we had two good societies, the Theological and the Missionary. Practical experience in the Pleasance opened one's eyes to the terribly harsh and sordid conditions in which many of the poor still lived and at the same time showed us the quiet and uncomplaining courage of the majority. To return from such surroundings usually left one with a salutary sense of moral discomfort and a realisation that there were many injustices in our national life. It was at evening service, on 1 January 1922, that I preached my first sermon in our Highland village, Nethy Bridge.

What did the time at the Divinity College give me? It gave me a sense that behind the changing generations the Church stretched back through the centuries to a unique divine Person. It gave me also a continuing interest in theology, the attempt to apprehend, however dimly, those great spiritual realities to which Christianity witnesses. More than that, it gave me an increasing longing to move from preparation to practice, to translate theology into language plain and appealing enough to draw others nearer "to Him Who is the Lord of all good life." I have felt for many years, and feel no less strongly today, that what was lacking was a period of residence in community. Education for the ministry is more academic than practical; it should also be a time for the formation of spiritual life. More could be done to help students if, at least for a few months, they lived together in one place where life would be centred on the chapel and academic studies carried on in an atmosphere of prayer, where individual needs could be met by wise pastoral counselling and strengthened by Holy Communion. It would send men out into the parish ministry with stronger inner resources.

It was about this time that an event occurred which considerably affected our life as a family. My sister, Constance, had gradually become friendly with members of the Lothian family and had been attending Roman Catholic churches. She finally decided to receive instruction and be admitted to the Roman Catholic Church. This decision came as a great shock to my father because at that time the differences between Protestant and Catholic were much more keenly felt. There was little interchange and almost none of the mutual understanding which prevails today. A convert to Roman Catholicism was inevitably separated in some degree from other members of the family at the deepest level.

I tried to dissuade my sister, but her mind was made up. She entered on a new pattern of life and never afterwards lived with us at home for more than occasional periods. But the change in no way altered our personal affection and, once he had got over the initial shock, my father accepted the situation with his usual large charity of judgement. My sister entered a convent for a time, but found that she had no vocation, but through the years she has used her varied gifts in the service of her Church with great joy and devotion. This unexpected happening brought home to me the realisation that there are many different gates into the city of God; that different communions within the one Universal Church have different insights and traditions; and that we all have much to learn from one another. To me the most appealing features of the Roman Catholic communion are the discipline of its devotional life and the wealth of its devotional literature.

2

Aberdeen

After completing my course at New College I was invited to become assistant minister in the historic charge of "Free St George's" in Edinburgh. At that time there were no strict rules about serving a probationary year before ordination, but it was clearly wise to have a period of pastoral apprenticeship under some experienced senior minister. St George's United Free Church was a large congregation with a long and distinguished tradition. It numbered among its members many men outstanding in different fields, academic, legal, and medical, and many prominent in business and commerce. It could look back on a succession of preachers whose names were known throughout Scotland and who attracted large congregations. Through the ministry of men of the highest moral and spiritual character and with gifts of unusual literary and rhetorical speech, St George's exercised wide influence.

It was therefore with feelings of mingled awe and expectation that I prepared to take up my duties as assistant minister to the Reverend Dr James Black, then at the height of his power and greatly loved. St George's was at that time an outstanding example of the cult of certain churches known for the eloquence and appeal of their preachers. These churches were almost always well filled. The evening service drew visitors from far and wide. It was a stimulating sight to see, Sunday after Sunday at 7 p.m., a queue some fifty or sixty feet in length and then, when the service began, to look round a church filled to capacity, some worshippers seated in the aisles and even on the pulpit steps. And Dr Black himself with his sensitive features, striking presence, and vibrant voice was, at his best, a moving and dramatic preacher. Perhaps fortunately the day of the "popular preacher" seems to have passed. It was a slightly artificial phenomenon, not acceptable in this more critical and questioning age.

As a very junior and inexperienced person I was seldom commanded to preach in St George's, but I was usually called to take some part in the services, leading the prayers or reading the lessons and occasionally giving a talk to the children. My principal duty was that of pastoral visiting. One of the weaknesses in the training for the ministry in Scotland at that time, and I think still, is that insufficient guidance is given in pastoral care. The young minister, academically well equipped, is sent out with little preparation for this important work. Visiting in different homes and meeting all sorts and conditions of people was of the greatest value and taught me much. Occasionally it proved formidable and communication was difficult. I was not in any sense over-worked, but, with the arrogance of youth, I had become critical of certain aspects of the life and work of St George's. Its standards of success seemed to me to be questionable. Its financial affluence was almost alarming. And an atmosphere of unconscious complacency was disturbing. Added to all this was a growing longing to have a parish and responsibilities of one's own. So that I began to look forward to the ending of my year's engagement and the new responsibilities ahead.

But first it was necessary to discover if any parish would give me a call. I had already had two tentative approaches, but both had come too early for me. About this time my father's health declined and the doctor firmly advised me that he must bring his ministry at North Berwick to an end. It was decided that he should come and make his home with me. At that moment the small United Free Church in Old Aberdeen became vacant. I was invited to preach, first unofficially in a neighbouring church and then officially as sole nominee, and was unanimously elected. I felt, and feel not less in looking back, how providentially I was led to a place in which both my father and I found remarkable happiness and fulfilment for the next few years.

Saying goodbye to North Berwick was not easy. My father accepted it quietly and calmly. My sister came from London, where she was living at that time, and she and I spent the last few days together, packing clothes, choosing some books to be given away, and saying goodbye. We had never known any other home. We determined to leave all the rooms as we had always known them, with a fire burning in the little drawing room and flowers on the tables; and so we simply locked the front door and drove away.

On Thursday, 14 May 1925, I was ordained and inducted by the presbytery of Aberdeen to my first parish and the same evening a meeting of welcome was held when I was presented with pulpit robes and academic hood and bands. Even now I can remember the frightening sense of loneliness and responsibility which seized me during the next few days, left to my own resources with all the care of a congregation. There was the daunting prospect of having to prepare two sermons every week, and the constant sub-consciousness of one's own spiritual inadequacy. Fears and anxieties soon began to be dissipated. So far as preaching was concerned, I soon began to discover the endless riches of the Bible. As for the duty of visiting, I was gradually caught up in the fascination of the pastoral relationship.

My father was immensely happy. He was a graduate of King's College and for him it was a return to familiar scenes. There is still a unique and unspoilt charm about Old Aberdeen. The old College buildings with the small quadrangle, the lovely chapel surmounted by its crown; the narrow cobbled streets, the Spittal, College Bounds, and the High Street, with their courtyards and closes and red-pantiled houses, leading up to the diminutive but dignified Town House; the great fourteenth century Cathedral Church of St Machar, the Chanonry, once the precinct of the Canons, now of university professors; and just northwards the quiet noble river Don, making its last spectacular bend before reaching the sea — all combine to compose a setting of unusual interest and beauty.

The congregation to which I had been called was an ideal size for a first ministry. It numbered about four hundred communicants and a good many children and was representative of all classes. The senior elder was Sir George Adam Smith, a distinguished Old Testament scholar and Principal of Aberdeen University, loved and revered in his own city and highly esteemed in academic circles across the world. He and his wife entertained charmingly and generously and Chanonry Lodge was a house in which one could meet interesting people from many lands. He never failed in support of the church; and on Sundays in term when he had to attend the University Chapel in the morning he would often come to evening service, sitting with members of his family in the back seat. Among other members of the kirk session were granite merchants, shop-keepers, a joiner, a painter, a chartered accountant, and one or two tradesmen. All were at one in their desire to give their service to the church. At session meetings there was frank discussion and keen argument, but we respected each other's opinions and were on friendliest personal terms.

My first duty, as I saw it, was to make proper personal acquaintance with the office-bearers and their families and then with all the congregation by pastoral visits to every home. A minister can only really come to know those committed to his care if he sees them in their own homes and family circles. He then becomes a friend. Occasionally visits were a little stiff and conversation difficult. People in the north are reserved, but once they have given their friendship it is given wholeheartedly. Even now there are many homes there in which I could count upon a welcome as kind and warm as in those far off days.

The other central duty of my life was preaching. When a preacher climbs the steps of a pulpit he sees before him a strangely varied group of people; and he has to speak to them. About what? About life in the light of the truth given to us in the Christian Gospel; Good News about a matchless life once lived in Galilee, about a Man through whose every word and action truth and love shone, about that same Man on a cross meeting the forces of evil and overcoming them by forgiveness and compassion, about an empty tomb in a garden on the first Easter morning, proclaiming the victory of goodness and life over death. But even when fortified by that tremendous message he is confronted by the question of how at all adequately to communicate it to that mixed group.

Almost invariably, according to age old tradition, the preacher begins by choosing a passage from the Bible, from whose pages countless men and women have heard the Word of God speaking to their needs in comfort and guidance. His task is to interpret the truths so that his hearers will listen and understand and respond, and go out spiritually cheered and strengthened. I used to pray in the vestry that, by the help of God, at least one hearer might be helped by the sermon of that day.

It was during my early months in Old Aberdeen that I began to realise that one of the primary essentials in preaching is simplicity of style, though not of thought. At the university we have cultivated a good and somewhat pedantic prose; the sooner we discard this in the pulpit, the better. The duty of the preacher is to speak in such a way that the simplest present may understand and find help. The Master Himself showed us how it is possible to speak on the profoundest themes in simple and homely language. Regularly every Sunday morning a pew near the front in a side aisle was occupied by a fine working man, his wife, and four children. John Cowie was a carter of meagre education but of upright character and strong faith. My father, who sat nearby, as we took our usual walk before lunch would say to me, "Well, that sermon was of no value to John Cowie this morning. You lost his attention after the first few minutes." On other occasions he would say, "I think you had John Cowie with you the whole time when you were preaching today." My father was a very wise person; throughout all the years of my ministry I have tried to remember his counsel about simplicity in preaching.

A minister is expected to be carefully prepared when he goes into the pulpit. For many people the hour in church on Sunday mornings is almost the only time in the week when they are invited to lift their thoughts to spiritual realities, and the sermon ought to provide for this. Throughout my whole ministry I have tried to keep the mornings free for theological reading and sermon writing. At that time one is fresher in mind and less liable to outside demands.

The United Free Church in Old Aberdeen had separated from St Machar's Cathedral in 1843 at the Disruption. Although well built, it was plain to the point of austerity. Its furnishings consisted of a good sized pulpit, a very small communion table, a harmonium, chairs for the choir, and rows of pews in varnished pine. I was anxious to have the church more attractively furnished; but we were relatively poor. However, I have always found that there are those who are glad to make gifts of a personal kind, often in memory of some dearly loved member of their family. When a greatly respected member, Dr Peter Mitchell, died, his wife and children wanted to make a gift in his memory and gladly responded to the suggestion of a lectern. I obtained for them from a distinguished architect a charming and dignified design. It added to the beauty of the church; even more important, it made it more easy for me to ask different members to share in the service by reading a lesson. This was usually done at first by one of the elders, but gradually younger men also read at the evening service. Another such gift was a font. Formerly the baptismal bowl sat in a bracket attached to one edge of the pulpit. After vows had been made the father held up the child and the minister leaned over the pulpit and administered the sacrament.

Further improvement which involved more discussion was the removal of pews at the east end of the church to make a children's chapel. A brightly coloured rug was provided and some small chairs. Attractive books were available. The whole was planned to give children a place of their own in God's house and to make them feel at home. Attendance in some rather cheerless hall does little to give children any sense of the splendour of God and the wonder at the heart of all true religion.

Ecclesiastically, our nearest neighbour was the great Cathedral Church of St Machar, standing in its quiet churchyard with two massive granite towers. On the south lay the Chanonry where in olden days stood the houses of the canons. Northwards it commanded a fine view of the Don before it reached the old Brig o' Balgownie and the open sea. Its congregation numbered some 3,000 communicants; its parish extended far beyond the city into farm lands and woods. For long it had been a collegiate charge. When I first went to Old Aberdeen the senior minister was Dr John Macgilchrist who had done splendid work in the great shipbuilding parish of Govan on the Clyde. He gave me a most kind and generous welcome at a garden party in the grounds of his manse. Dignified, conservative, and kind, if a little formidable, he belonged to the older school of Scottish churchmanship.

I had only been in Old Aberdeen some two years when circumstances made it possible to cement more warmly the relationship with our large neighbour. Considerable repairs to the Cathedral were needed and there was the prospect of holding Sunday services in a rather bleak church hall. With the agreement of our kirk session I invited the Cathedral congregation to join us in worship in our small church. To my delight, and somewhat to my surprise, the invitation was gratefully accepted.

I suggested to Dr Macgilchrist that he and I should preach on alternate Sunday mornings and that he should preach on our first Sunday together. There was only one awkward feature. I had been attempting to lead my own people into a better observance of the Christian Year; and had announced that on the four Sundays of Advent we should be thinking of the great traditional themes of "The Four Last Things: Death, Judgement, Hell, Heaven." I decided that I would not break the series, but would take my courage in both hands and ask Dr MacGilchrist to accept the arrangement.

I was duly ushered into his study and with some trepidation made my request. With characteristic courtesy he agreed. Finally he asked me the fateful question, "Then what will be my subject next Sunday?" I could only answer in one word, "Hell". There was a strained pause. He sat back in his large armchair, then said, "My dear boy, strange to say in all my ministry I have never preached a sermon on Hell, and I don't feel I could compose such a sermon now, when I seldom write anything new." He went on to insist that I must do it myself. As a result, old Miss Penelope Pirie, daughter of a former Principal of Aberdeen University, meeting a mutual friend in the Chanonry a few days later, said "Did you ever hear such a discourse as the young minister gave us last Sunday? It was a terrible thing."

In a short time I became concerned about the need for keeping churches open and accessible on weekdays. A church should surely be kept open as a place of quiet in which it is possible to enjoy a few minutes of prayer and find an atmosphere of peace. I felt so strongly the need to rethink our traditional Scottish custom of the locked church that I raised the matter at Aberdeen presbytery. The proposal was on the whole favourably received and the motion to consider keeping churches open accepted. When I raised it at my own kirk session various practical difficulties were mentioned. "Who would open and shut the church? And would he have to be paid?" The answer was simple, for I would do it myself. My commitment to this involved little inconvenience because my manse was exactly opposite the church. Actually the duty became a source of spiritual profit. The times had been left to my own discretion, and I used to make the opening after breakfast, say my morning prayers there and do some devotional reading. Usually I was alone. The short period of solitude in the little church that I loved was a delightful prelude to the day's work, and the practice continued through all the remaining years in Old Aberdeen.

Just outside the door I had a simple notice board bearing the words, "This house of God is open daily for prayer and meditation." It was a shock to find one morning that the board had been rudely torn down and carried away. A group of students, returning late from a party, were passing. One of them, in hilarious mood, seeing the notice board, tore it from its post and carried it in triumph to his lodgings. When his landlady roused him she pointed sternly to the dressing table and asked, "What might that be?" Well she might, for in very strange surroundings it announced, "This house of God is open daily for prayer and meditation". The notice board was returned with suitable apologies.

From the first days of Christianity the followers of Christ observed the "Breaking of Bread" on the Lord's Day. It was a rite given to the Church by our Lord Himself. Although in the late Middle Ages the bad practice of non-communicating attendance at Mass became prevalent, yet at least Mass was said in all churches on Sundays. "Once a week at the very least," Calvin said, "the Lord's Supper should be celebrated in the Christian congregation." Owing to the conservatism of the civil authorities in Geneva he was unable to realise his ideal, and was compelled "for the sake of peace" to accept a quarterly celebration: at Christmas, Easter, Pentecost, and Harvest. It was this custom which was brought to Scotland by John Knox, but his own teaching was profoundly sacramental and in the Book of Common Order of 1564 a monthly celebration was recommended. Instead it was found possible to have a celebration only once or at most twice a year in many parishes; and this custom of infrequent communion continues, leading to a false conception of the place of the Sacrament in the life of the Church as a whole and of the individual Christian.

Only after some experience as a minister did I begin to read and think more deeply about this. And the more carefully I thought, the more convinced I felt that here was a point of spiritual weakness. These feelings I tried to express in an article on "Holy Communion" in the April number of *The Record* in 1927 and in a letter to *The Scotsman*. Several of my session were very conservative, but I knew that they had generously given me their trust. I explained the place of the Lord's Supper as central in the life of the Chuch not as a rare occasion but as a strengthening of the Christian life, bringing comfort and joy, and available as often as possible. A long discussion followed and it was unanimously decided that there should be a celebration on the first Sunday of every month after the ordinary morning service. This response gave me great happiness. The monthly communion was never largely attended, the numbers usually being between thirty and fifty; and of course we continued to hold the great congregational communion twice in the year.

Pastoral relationships brought many enriching experiences. Once the widow of a fisherman in a cottage close to the sand dunes north of the Don spoke of the cross and its meaning. Her eyes lit up with understanding, and in about three simple sentences she described the essential meaning and message of the Atonement in a way which might well have been envied by many theologians. In my diary of 12 November 1927 occurs the entry, "Went to see old Mr Rose, who is dying. He was very low, but recognised me, and smiled when I repeated John 14 v. 1-3, and other passages...... Sunday 13 November: Went out to the Bridge of Don to the Roses and was just in time. He died five minutes after I got there, very peacefully, at 7.55." Such experiences gave a depth to one's own outlook on life. Looking back now after many years, I am impressed by the quiet and uncomplaining courage shown by so many in face of the mysteries of suffering and illness and death, and especially when fortified by Christian faith.

Old Aberdeen had something of the atmosphere of a village. One was in touch with all sections of a delightfully mixed community. In the academic circle there was a good deal of social life, rather formal little luncheon and dinner parties, tea parties and tennis parties. At any dinner party the men were expected to wear dinner jackets and often long coats. If one should call in the middle of the morning on that wonderful old lady, Miss Penelope Pirie, within a few minutes a parlour maid would come into the drawing room bringing a tray on which were a plate of plum cake and a decanter of Madeira. After which would flow a conversation of sparkling anecdote on times past and pungent comment on times present.

One of the most delightful functions was held in the grounds of Chanonry Lodge, the residence of the Principal of the University. In the middle of the lawn nearest to the house stood a magnificent old cherry tree or, as we call it in Scotland, a Gean. In late May or early June its marvellous display of white blossom created almost the effect of a huge candelabrum. Every year Sir George and Lady Adam Smith gave a garden party to celebrate not only the beauty of the splendid ancient tree, but the return of summer after the long northern winter.

I was fortunate enough to be elected to membership of the North East Theological Club which met once a month during the winter. It numbered about twenty ministers and all the members of the Divinity Faculty. Each member was called on in turn to read a paper, followed by discussion. The talk and fellowship were stimulating; and if younger members were sometimes over-awed by superior scholarship it encouraged one to keep up one's reading.

No less stimulating was a project of open air speaking in the summer months. It sprang from the conviction that since a great many working class men never came into a church, some attempt ought to be made to proclaim the Gospel to them in some less conventional and more familiar setting. A rather flimsy lorry was hired and drawn by a horse to the centre of the Castlegate where there was ample space. The horse was unyoked and the minister climbed on the lorry and gradually drew an audience. It was an alarming experience to a novice. Often one had a crowd of some eighty or a hundred. When my turn came to speak I was irritated to find the lorry extremely unsteady. I assumed that it had been carelessly placed where the cobblestones were uneven, but glancing down I discovered that it was my own legs that were shaking. Soon after one began the nervousness vanished and one was absorbed in one's subject and the determination to keep the crowd which could turn on their heels in boredom and walk away. Questions often roved far and called for alertness and tolerance. Always there were some who were anxious to trip up the speaker. Answers had to be straightforward and brief; but questioning appealed, and often the speaker had to draw the occasion to a close as twilight came on. Even among those who call themselves agnostics or secularists there are many who "are not far from the Kingdom of God."

On Sunday 30 October 1927 I engaged for the first time in a very different kind of witness, for I had been asked to conduct a short broadcast service. It was taken in the B.B.C. studio in Belmont Street at 8 o'clock. My diary records the bare statement: "Put on my gown, cassock, and hood, to get the atmosphere of worship. Preached on 'The City had twelve gates'." This was the first of many occasions on which I have had the privilege of preaching through radio or television. Little did one realise in those early days what an enormous part broadcasting would play in the life of the nation.

I had always read widely, having been specially influenced by the robust writing of Thomas Carlyle and Robert Browning, by the poetry of Milton, Dante, and Francis Thompson, and by the great Russian novelists, Tolstoy, Turgenev, and Dostoevsky. At the university reading, chiefly in history and philosophy, was dictated by class work. At New College both the lectures and the prescribed books reflected the Reformed outlook. As a result, I had done very little reading of Roman Catholic or Anglican theology or devotional writings. During my years at Old Aberdeen I began to widen the range of my reading. Among books which made an impression on me were the Bampton Lectures, *The Vision of God* by Kenneth E. Kirk, Bishop of Oxford, *Essays Catholic and Critical*, a volume of notable essays by Anglican scholars and a striking and beautiful book, which appeared in 1927, *The Spirit of Catholicism*, by a distinguished Roman Catholic, Karl Adam, and Rudolf Otto's great book, *The Idea of the Holy*. I also read and used for my personal devotions in Lent one year the *Spiritual Exercises* of Ignatius Loyola. Another work, read then for the first time but used continually through the years since was Lancelot Andrewes' *Private Devotions*. But above all the *Essays and Addresses* and the *Letters* of Baron von Hügel moved and excited me, both theologically and spiritually, and in many ways transformed my whole religious outlook, with his constant emphasising of the interweaving of nature and super-nature, the homely and the mysterious. These and similar books took me into a wider field than I had until then discovered. In all of them, I became aware of the sense of the transcendent, the otherness or unlikeness of God, the supernatural element underlying or breaking through the Christian Gospel and the writings of both the Old Testament and the New Testament at every point. In all these so varied writers I noticed also again and again the emphasis on the importance of the inner life and of worship and prayer.

Gradually I grew more convinced that in the life and tradition of our Scottish Reformed Church there was something lacking. It was the same feeling which I had had, though less consciously, in my final year at New

College. In our Church there has been continuously, generation after generation, a profound interest in theology, and a strong belief in the importance of preaching. Through the Shorter Catechism and the knowledge of the Scriptures children must be brought up in sound doctrine. But sound doctrine is no substitute for prayer. Belief in God is not equivalent to communion with God; and in our Reformed tradition there has been little attempt at the cultivation of the inner life or training in the practice of prayer.

After much discussion of this subject my neighbour and friend, the Reverend Melville Dinwiddie, then minister of St Machar's Cathedral, and I decided to try to make some small contribution to the meeting of this problem by arranging a retreat for ministers, a thing unknown in our Church at that time, in which an opportunity would be offered, not for conference, but for meditation, self-examination, silence, and prayer. We decided to begin on a very small and tentative basis. Invitations were sent privately only to a few men upon whose interest and sympathy we could count, although they reflected different traditions of churchmanship. The place of meeting chosen was Bonskeid House, a secluded mansion-house which belonged to the Barbour family but which had been rented to the Young Men's Christian Association. Standing in a quiet glen between Pitlochry and Blair Atholl, surrounded by magnificent trees and hills, and with the turbulent river Tummel flowing through a rocky channel close to the house, it had a setting of natural beauty and an atmosphere of peace and privacy which seemed ideal for our purpose.

A group of eight of us gathered there for the first retreat in September 1928. Meeting on a Monday evening, we dispersed again on the Friday morning. Each day began with a celebration of holy communion, and the time was divided between corporate devotions, private prayer, addresses, discussion, and regular periods of silence. We, there "all of one mind and one heart", were conscious of being spiritually refreshed and enriched; and felt that we had discovered something new and valuable in the silence and the opportunity which it gave for meditation and self-examination.

There was, however, one important thing missing. We had converted one of the rooms in the house into a temporary chapel; but we felt that, if possible, we must in future meet in some place where we could hold our celebrations of holy communion and prayers in a church rather than a house. Perthshire seemed ideally central. In the little township of Dunkeld was the small old Cathedral standing in its own quiet grounds on the bank of the river Tay. The parish minister, when approached, willingly gave permission for us to have the use of the church. And the factor of the Atholl estates kindly allowed us to use the beautiful grounds along the river opening out of the Cathedral precincts. We were able to secure accommodation in the Royal Hotel nearby.

Here was the ideal situation for a retreat. The number of invitations sent out was increased, although always privately and without any publicity. Some men came once or twice and did not return. Others came year after year. The average, and perhaps ideal, number was between twenty and twentyfive. Each year there were a few new men. There was a good organ in the Cathedral, and among us there were always one or two musicians such as George T. Wright, Roy Hogg, Harry Miller, and Ian Forbes. The various duties were divided among the members present so that there was always a rich diversity of thought and approach.

Soon it was decided that the best time for holding the retreat was shortly after Easter, so as to provide an opportunity for spiritual rest and renewal at the end of the winter's work. In 1936 it was resolved to found a society under the name of "The Fellowship of Dunkeld", membership being open to any who had attended a retreat. The aim of the Fellowship was defined as "to promote amongst the members and any whom they influence or who may join them hereafter, a deeper experimental knowledge of God the Father, in Jesus Christ; a more faithful and self-denying service in His kingdom, and more Christ-like relationships to one another." Members of the society bound themselves to a simple daily act of meditation, remembrance, and intercession.

Owing to the difficulties of war-time no retreats were held from 1941 to 1946. But, except for the interval, the annual retreat has been held continuously up to the present time. In it we have not only discovered the unique value of silence in the spiritual life, but have also found what Cyril Hepher called "the fellowship of silence", so that in silence we are not separated from others, but can often experience friendship at a deeper level than in speech. We live in an age of conferences on every conceivable subject, but a retreat offers something quite different. It reminds us of what Archbishop Anthony Bloom describes as "the importance of sitting and doing nothing in front of God... to place ourselves in the Presence of God and to remain there without trying to escape." Perhaps it is because the Dunkeld Retreat has attempted to meet this need that it has continued for more than forty years.

3

Aberdeen to Dundee

By far the most important event in the religious life of Scotland during the first half of this century was the reunion of two great branches of the Church. The Disruption of 1843 had brought about a cleavage in religious loyalties which affected the whole population of the country from north to south and east to west. The controversy concerned the vitally important principle of the freedom of the Church in matters spiritual and ecclesiastical and involved the whole complex problem of the relationship of Church and State. It had at first engendered bitterly antagonistic feelings on both sides and, in practical terms, had resulted in the building of new churches and manses throughout the whole country for those who felt in conscience compelled to leave the Established Church. The new Free Church still claimed pastoral responsibility for all the people, which meant that in every parish there were two churches, the members of which had few communications with one another.

Although it had its heroic aspects in voluntary sacrifice and loyalty to conscience, the situation was religiously tragic. And it gave much pain to all serious Christian people and especially to the leaders on both sides. The first sign of hope came with the abolition of patronage in 1874, which at once seemed to open the door to better understanding. Gradually relations between the two Churches became warmer. Various informal conversations and exchanges of views took place. But it was not until 1908 that the General Assembly of the Church of Scotland issued an invitation to the United Free Church "to confer in a friendly and generous spirit on the present ecclesiastical situation in Scotland, and to consider how a larger measure of Christian fellowship and co-operation could be brought about, so as to prepare the way for union, for which so many were hoping and praying." The invitation was accepted, and large and representative committees were set up on both sides.

Important and complicated problems had to be solved. On the side of the Established Church it was felt that the concept of a National Church must be preserved, and that some kind of relationship with the State was of great value. On the side of the United Free Church there was an unswerving insistence that the freedom of the Church must be recognised and secured for all time in matters of doctrine, worship, and government. To reconcile and hold together these two important principles required many years of conference and discussion. When finally agreement was reached it was necessary to persuade Parliament to make the necessary changes. This was achieved when in 1925 The Church of Scotland (Properties and Endowments) Bill became law.

At last, in May 1929, the Basis and Plan of Union was approved in both General Assemblies; and it was decided that the act of union should take place in October. My father and I were both members of the General Assembly that year, and made our way to Edinburgh to join in the consummation and celebration of the long awaited event. Imaginative plans had been made. On the morning of the chosen day a procession of ministers and elders of the Established Church began to move slowly from the Tolbooth Church down the Lawnmarket, while another similar procession moved from New College and up the Mound. The two processions met at the top of the High Street, greeted each other, merged with each other, and then entered the High Kirk of St Giles' for a great act of united thanksgiving, prayer, and dedication. Later in the day, in a huge hall, with hundreds of both Churches present, the union was officially constituted, creating once again a single Church of Scotland, a Church both national and free.

My father and I walked side by side in the procession from New College, deeply moved and happy, and conscious that we were taking part in an event which would transform the whole religious life of Scotland. Many readjustments, both in thinking and in ecclesiastical practice, would have to be made. Many new problems would have be be dealt with in the years ahead. But the old division in the religious life and work of the country, with all its jealousies, rivalries, and suspicions, had been brought to an end. And now we could together use the combined resources of both Churches in planning, in practical service, and in finance to promote the spiritual good of Scotland.

Although I regretted, and still regret, never having had a country parish, my years in Old Aberdeen were wonderfully full, varied, and happy. I became deeply attached to the little township, with its distinctive personality, its narrow High Street, its cobbled alleys and courtyards, its solid stone built houses, its reserved and yet friendly people. My own congregation was large enough to keep me fully occupied and yet small enough to enable me to know all its members individually and intimately. Doubtless I made many mistakes in those early years of my ministry. There were occasional difficult incidents and difficult personal relationships, chiefly in connection with certain changes I made in the worship and the furnishings of the church, perhaps without careful enough explanation. I learned then the important lesson that any such innovations should be explained with the greatest courtesy and care to the congregation, and that when so introduced they will almost always be accepted.

My greatest good fortune during those years was the companionship, wisdom, and guidance of my dear father. I could discuss every problem with him, and rely if not always upon his agreement yet always upon his sympathy and affection. He enjoyed his daily walks, either down to the sand dunes and the sea or through the Aulton where he knew and talked to almost everyone. And on days when I was free, we would drive out into the open country in different directions; sometimes northwards through the rich farm lands of Buchan, a countryside almost without trees but with wide far stretching views and magnificent skyscapes; or up the coast by the sand dunes of Newburgh where hundreds of terns nested in relative peace, and on by the wild sea beaten cliffs of the Bullers of Buchan and the little fishing communities where for generations brave and hardy men had carried on their dangerous occupation among the storms of the North Atlantic; or sometimes we turned inland, driving up the line of the beautiful river Don by Inverurie and Monymusk and Echt, with the splendid solitary shoulder of Benachie standing up amongst the surrounding flat moorland. At other times we took the roads which followed the famous river Dee, with its even more spectacular scenery and its romantic royal associations. Aberdeenshire is a county of wonderfully varied beauty, in which one can almost always escape from noise and crowds, if one knows its remoter corners. Sometimes my father and I on such off days would stop for lunch at some small quiet inn, but more often we had a picnic lunch, sitting on the heather or on the bank of some small stream, our desultory talk varying from current affairs of Church and State to faraway days of his boyhood on his father's farm or his student days at King's College.

My father was one of those people who contrive to grow old gracefully, with no complaints at failing powers but rather with an increased contentment and tranquillity, so that, in the words of St Paul, "though the outward part of his nature was being worn down, his inner life was refreshed from day to day". In the early months of 1930 his strength began to decline and his memory to become confused. My sister returned home to help look after him; and in the last weeks we were all greatly fortified by the almost daily visits of his friend, Dr David Cairns, Principal of the Theological College, whose wise wide outlook on life and whose deep spiritual insight were closely akin to my father's. The end came very quietly, and he passed peacefully in sleep into the nearer presence of the God whom he had for so long reverenced and loved and tried to serve.

The funeral was at North Berwick, the scene of his long ministry. To my sorrow, I was ill and in bed and unable to travel, but my sister and other relations were there. As they drove through the familiar High Street the blinds had been pulled down in every house and shop in honour and affection. His body was laid to rest in the cemetery just below the great mass of the Law which, in younger days, he had so often climbed and from whose summit one looks out southwards across the rich East Lothian fields and northwards to the Firth of Forth with its islands and lighthouses and ever changing seascape.

An extract from a weekly paper gives the impression made upon an outsider by my father's personality and preaching, "If he is a fair sample of her ministers one can understand how it was that the United Free Church held staunchly together in the recent troublous times, and how the ministers and the united Church are a powerful force for good in the Scotland of today. ...a tall, spare, lithe figure with a shrewd, kindly Scottish face, very human, one to whom one could go for counsel or sympathy; a clean shaven face, and iron gray hair. The service had not well begun till one is caught by the simple, reverential tone and the intense earnestness of the man. His prayers convey the conviction of a man "far ben" with his Maker, as the old Scottish saying was; he talks as a man talks to his close friend. All of the sermons show Scottish evangelicalism of today as influenced by German theology. This man is evidently a scholar and a thinker, who reads widely, but has yet never lost his old bearings. He holds in the main the old Gospel of his fathers even if, in some ways, he holds it with a difference. ...Mr Davidson is a man in the direct succession to Chalmers and Guthrie and Candlish and others."

My father's death left a great blank in my life and in our manse. It also brought inevitable domestic changes. Perhaps fortunately, our house parlourmaid Mary had left to be married. For various reasons it became necessary to part with our cook, Margaret. Instead I engaged an elderly and rather formidable housekeeper, Mrs Christie. She looked after me with great efficiency, but expected much greater punctuality for meal times, and did not approve of visitors casually invited at short notice. She had a small house of her own near the Bridge of Dee at the other side of the town; and did not hesitate from time to time to hint that it was only as a considerable favour that she consented to live in Old Aberdeen and look after my manse.

But what above all made the changed atmosphere at home was of course the absence of my father's companionship, so that I felt a loneliness which until then I had never known. Fortunately there were many kind and congenial friends nearby who asked one out to lunch or dinner from time to time; and there were several houses to which I could go without any formality. One of the most congenial of all neighbours was John Laird, Professor of Moral Philosophy, with whom I had many enjoyable contests, physically on Balgownie golf course and verbally in his study on winter evenings. I have never known anyone who more obviously enjoyed argument for its own sake as a kind of intellectual game. His charming wife sat by, doing her embroidery and listening with quizzical amusement. Another near neighbour and friend was G.D. Henderson, Professor of Ecclesiastical History. Although modern in some of his ideas, such as the rightness of admitting women to the ministry, in his general church outlook he was a Moderate who might have walked straight out of the eighteenth century, tolerant in judgement and suspicious of any form of enthusiasm, so that my conversation with him also often developed into delightful and stimulating argument.

Happy as I had been in Old Aberdeen, my mind began gradually turning to the possibility of a change to some slightly larger charge. My name had in fact been considered for a vacant parish in Crieff, but someone else was preferred; and I reached the conclusion that there was still work for me to do in the northern city which I had come to love. In the spring of 1932 however there came a completely unexpected invitation to allow myself to be made sole nominee for the *quoad sacra* parish of St Enoch's, Dundee. I knew nothing of this charge, but the moderator in the vacancy gave me a good deal of information about its past history and present opportunities, and the invitation was very cordial. It seemed to offer the rather wider sphere of the ministry for which I had hoped. I therefore gladly agreed to preach as sole nominee, and was duly elected.

I said goodbye to my parishioners and friends in Old Aberdeen with much sadness, and also with countless affectionate and grateful memories. On Monday 18 April the presbytery of Dundee inducted me to the charge of St Enoch's, and on the Tuesday evening I was very kindly welcomed at a social gathering of the congregation. It is, I suppose, never easy to move to a completely new environment; but a clergyman is peculiarly fortunate, because he comes to his new sphere of work not as a lonely stranger but as one who can count upon the friendly welcome of his congregation who have themselves called him. For me, the prospect was full of promise. St Enoch's was a handsome church, well furnished, and with a splendid situation in the Nethergate, one of the main streets in the centre of the city. The communicant membership was about 700 and was representative of all classes. The manse was a spacious and comfortable house at the western end of Magdalene Green, with a magnificent outlook up the wide river Tay across Invergowrie Bay to the low hills of Fife.

I was now relieved of any financial anxieties with a stipend of £620 per annum and the rates and taxes and telephone expenses paid by the congregation. At first I engaged a very reliable housekeeper who arrived with her beloved sheep dog, and I thought she might be with me for many years; but her aged father became ill and she had to return to Orkney to look after him. I then decided to try and find two younger maids and was lucky beyond all expectation. In August Flora Cant came as cook and stayed on through all changes, even the great change of my marriage, becoming a devoted and well loved friend of the family and only leaving us, 35 years later, when death suddenly called her away. Her friendship and help have been one of the major blessings of our life. At the same time a young house parlour maid, Annie, came and stayed with me until she married some years later.

Dundee, then a town of some 160,000 population, was almost completely new to me. It has a splendid situation on the Tay with houses and shops in terraces on the steeply rising land and culminating in the Law. Eastwards was the pleasant residential area of Broughty Ferry with its large villas and beautiful gardens, and, further east still, the sand dunes of Monifieth, Barry, and Carnoustie with their fine golf courses. As I studied the communicants' roll of St Enoch's and began to plan my pastoral visitation I discovered that there were members in almost every part of the city. I determined to try to visit every home once a year in addition to all the special visiting of old and ill people. This would at least keep me in touch with every family. It meant that visits could not be long, perhaps about half an hour, but in pastoral visitation there has to be great flexibility and the minister must never give any impression of haste, especially if the conversation is on any intimate or serious personal problem.

The staple industry of Dundee had long been the jute trade; and during the thirties there was a slump and many firms were experiencing great difficulties. Unemployment was widespread. Curiously enough, it was easier for women to find work; and in visiting I often found the strange and sad phenomenon of the father at home looking after the children and cooking dinner while the wife and mother was working in a factory. Many employers were deeply distressed. I remember the chairman of one large firm telling me that he had kept business going in his factory for many months at considerable loss until he was obliged at last to close down. For some time he felt the adjustment to idleness so difficult that he continued to go to his office simply to sit and read the newspaper.

I found great happiness in the services at St Enoch's. There was a splendid organ, the leading singers in the choir were paid, and there was a fine musical tradition. The church itself, though not beautiful, was devotional in character, and well furnished. From the outside it was a notable landmark with its two towers, the residence of many pigeons. The morning services were well attended and had an atmosphere of reverence. The evening services gradually improved and I tried to make them different in character. One winter we had a monthly series of addresses by well known laymen, Sir Leon Levison on "Christianity and Judaism", the Earl of Glasgow on "The Dangers of Communism," and my uncle, Colonel Quentin Agnew, on "Religion in the Army." Holy communion was celebrated only twice in the year but the Kirk Session allowed me to have a monthly celebration in addition. On summer evenings a great many people passed the doors of St Enoch's but few came into church. I suggested that after the ordinary evening service we should have some hymn singing and a brief act of worship in the small courtyard next to the pavement to appeal to the casual passer-by. Most members of the session thought the project undignified, but I joined other clergy in informal meetings at the West Port where we could count on a lively audience, some of them Communists, to listen and ask endless questions. I was also able to carry out a much fuller observance of the Christian Year. At Christmas time I procured a beautiful tree which was placed below the chancel steps. To light it, we used ordinary wax candles. I was astonished to receive a letter from one of our older members saying that she had never expected to see Popery in this form in St Enoch's and that never in future would she feel able to attend Christmas services. A long and friendly conversation persuaded her to change her views and to reconcile her to her new minister.

In Dundee I was fortunate to find myself in easy reach of several relations. A few miles along the Carse of Gowrie lived my cousins, Lord and Lady Kinnaird at Rossie Priory, and not far off my uncle, Colonel Agnew, and his wife. In both houses one was welcome at any time. Pastoral and other duties kept me busy in Dundee but it was often possible to find a few hours to escape into the country. On Sundays in summer I would drive out to Rossie after morning service arriving for lunch and a walk through the glen in the afternoon, returning in time for the evening service. My uncle Quentin was frail and could not walk far, but we enjoyed talking as we sat in their garden at Mill Hill with its wide view across the woods to the Tay. In those days large country houses still kept considerable state, with much entertaining and many servants. But it was the end of an era.

Among the memorable experiences of the years in Dundee was a first visit to Balmoral. Through the domestic chaplain, the minister of Crathie, I received a command to preach before His Majesty and to stay for a weekend at the castle. I received the invitation with mingled trepidation and delight. First and most perplexing was to choose a suitable subject and then to prepare it with proper brevity because, by the King's wish, it should not exceed twelve minutes.

In those days trains were still running from Aberdeen to Ballater. At Ballater station I was courteously greeted by the station master and escorted to a waiting royal car. The ten or twelve miles of road gave ever more lovely views of the Highland countryside with the river, the early autumn foliage of the woods, and the great jagged outline of Lochnagar in the distance. At the side door of Balmoral about 6 o'clock I was received by the equerry on duty and taken into the smoking room. Soon afterwards the domestic chaplain came to see me and discuss the arrangements for Sunday. Later I was escorted upstairs to dress for dinner. In those days the quarters reserved for a visiting minister were a spacious bedroom and a very pleasant sitting room in the tower. Dinner was not until 8.30, so there was ample time to have a bath, shave, and change.

Arrangements then were more formal than today. The footmen wore brass buttoned livery with breeches and stockings and there seemed a great many of them. As we waited in the drawing room before their Majesties joined us I was greatly comforted in my shyness by two things. The lady in waiting, Miss Jean Bruce, a member of the Balfour of Burleigh family, happened to be a great friend of one of my uncles and greeted me most charmingly. The other reassuring moment was when the Master of the Household, Sir Derek Keppel, as he then was, came up to me and said, "You will be sitting next to the Queen at dinner; but don't be in the least anxious about conversation, as some people seem to be. Be completely natural and talk to her as you would to any other lady."

A moment later the guests were lined up in a row, their Majesties came in and we were successively presented and then went in to dinner. Queen Mary was formidably regal and had it not been for Sir Derek Keppel's reassuring advice I should certainly have been tongue tied. As it was, conversation became easy and delightful. When the ladies left the dining room I was taken to sit with the King. He was also formidable, but refreshingly downright and blunt in his way of speaking. We discussed the immense number of people who congregated outside Crathie Church to see the Royal family. "Hundreds of those," he said, "have no intention of coming into church. If I had my way I would put a rope round the crowd and insist that they all contribute to the collection." After returning to the drawing room everyone remained standing until their Majesties retired.

On Sunday morning I was driven early to the church but already the crowds were gathering. The service was conducted by the parish minister, while the visiting minister read the lessons and preached. Speaking was easy as the church was small and completely full. I had chosen as my subject "The Simplicity of Christianity", the text being St. Matthew 11 v.5, and I think I kept within the allotted time. When we returned the King made some kindly appreciative remark and I felt thankful that the ordeal was over. In the afternoon Miss Bruce took me for a walk up the wooded hillside. In the evening their Majesties said farewell, though I did not leave till after breakfast the following day, carrying with me memories of a weekend full of kindness. I was honoured by a similar invitation next summer and since then I have had the privilege of preaching in Crathie and staying at Balmoral on some seven or eight occasions. In these later years one finds at Balmoral a greater informality but the same wonderful welcome and the same loyalty to the Christian faith and the Church.

4

Glasgow

I had only been in Dundee about two and a half years when an event occurred which changed all my expectations. The charge of Glasgow Cathedral become vacant. To my astonishment I received a letter from the session clerk, Gavin Boyd, saying that the vacancy committee would like to hear me preach. I replied that I would be preaching in the High Kirk of St Giles' on a Sunday in the near future. When the day came a message awaited me in the vestry saying that the vacancy committee would like to meet me afterwards. This was arranged, the vestry was put at our disposal, and many questions were asked and answered. A few days later I had a letter saying that a deputation hoped to see me at my manse. They were extremely kind and friendly and said that it was their unanimous wish that I should preach as sole nominee.

My predecessor in St Enoch's, Professor J.H.S. Burleigh, had only had a three years ministry there. I myself had had a ministry of less than three years. Would I be justified in leaving so soon? I resolved to call a meeting of the kirk session, tell them the facts, and leave myself in their hands. We had a full and frank discussion, at the end of which with great generosity, they expressed their opinion that the call to Glasgow was one that I could not refuse. A few weeks later, in November, I conducted morning and evening worship in the Cathedral and was elected.

These happenings gave me mixed feelings. I regretted leaving Dundee, but the call to Glasgow made me minister of the largest and most beautiful mediaeval church in Scotland, with a splendid liturgical and musical tradition and unique opportunities of influence. The prospect filled me with trepidation and exhilaration. It was a call in the true and deep sense of the word.

In mediaeval times the bishop had his residence close to the Cathedral. Since then the Cathedral had no manse, but each minister had to buy his own residence. I rather welcomed the duty of finding a house that appealed to me. A favourite cousin came to help. Many houses were available and prices were low. We could find nothing suitable near the Cathedral which was now almost completely surrounded by dilapidated tenements. Finally I decided on a tall narrow house of character, not far from the University, looking out on a small private garden, and with many windows since it stood at a corner, 69 Oakfield Avenue. It was larger than I needed, being three stories in height. As it stood on steeply sloping ground there was also a double basement, with a small garden behind. A large drawing room and dining room made entertaining easy. A good-sized bedroom and sitting room were available for the two maids, Flora and Annie, who had agreed to move with me to Glasgow. On the top floor I had my study and bedroom and my own bathroom, all adjoining, with refreshingly wide views and a sense of peace, being remote from the front door. I bought the house for £600.

On 30 January 1935 the presbytery of Glasgow inducted me into the charge of the Cathedral. As I walked slowly towards the church and suddenly saw its great spire coming to view above the surrounding roof-tops an almost overwhelming sense of responsibility swept over me, followed by a silent but intense prayer that I might be given the much needed strength to be equal to it. The responsibilities were heavy and formidable. There was the pastoral care of a congregation of about 1,200 communicant members scattered far and wide across the city. Beyond that, the Cathedral was the mother church of the city, and its minister was minister of Glasgow, having close relations with the town council, the Merchants' House, the Trades House, and many other institutes. Special services of all kinds were held in it, and on any occasion of national or civic significance when prayer was needed it was to the Cathedral that many people naturally turned. Here worship had been carried on for some seven hundred years; but the spot had been sacred even earlier as the burial place of the Celtic saint, Kentigern or Mungo, who died in 603.

The Cathedral stands on ground which slopes to the Molendinar Burn, and the architect took advantage of this to construct the eastern half at two levels, providing a crypt, or rather a lower church of spacious and beautiful design. In the centre of the crypt is the tomb of St Mungo. This long heritage gives a sense of continuity from the earliest days of Celtic Christianity.

During the Middle Ages the diocese grew in importance and became an archbishopric. The great church was richly furnished, and had at one time more than thirty altars and many canons and prebendaries. Although over three hundred feet in length, it is divided by a large stone screen or pulpitum which makes it possible to hold different kinds of services in the nave and choir. At the north east corner the mediaeval chapterhouse and sacristy survive, but unfortunately the two great western towers were demolished in the nineteenth century. Otherwise the church stands in its original dignity and grandeur, no addition having been made since the building of the Blackader Aisle in the early sixteenth century.

When the reformation took place in 1560 the liturgical customs of the Middle Ages were swept away, sacramental vessels and other treasures were taken to Paris, and none of the carved stalls or stained glass survived. The marvel is that the structure of the Cathedral itself survived undamaged. A new chapter opened. Government by presbyteries and kirk sessions replaced government by bishops. Forms of worship were simplified, prominence was given to preaching and teaching, and furnishings were of the plainest. In Glasgow the Cathedral became the parish church of the city. In the sad controversies of the seventeenth century and the apathy of the eighteenth little interest was taken in architectural beauty and neglect led to the decay of many of our older places of worship in Scotland.

Two tasks face a new minister in such a charge, to become acquainted with the kirk session and congregation, and to give careful thought to the services. Regular pastoral visitation began at once, but it would be months before I could visit every home. Fortunately I had the help of two excellent assistant ministers, the Rev. James Hay Hamilton and the Rev. George Innes. Every Monday morning we met in my study to discuss practical and pastoral problems. Then and in the following years this exchange of ideas and sharing of responsibilities with younger colleagues was immensely interesting and comforting. Their continuing friendship has meant much to me.

Each of the four large cities of Scotland has a personality of its own. Any generalization about a city the size of Glasgow can only be partially true, but I think all who have lived there would agree that it is a city of great vitality. One lived at the hub of Scotland's industrial life. Shipbuilding firms and great engineering firms of the Clyde bore names that were famous across the world. Something of their achievements and traditions has been told in the novels of George Blake. "Clyde-built" was still a phrase to denote unquestioned excellence. New developments in light industries were being encouraged.

In spite of a conscience about social needs, there was still an appalling shortage of good housing; thousands lived in dilapidated tenements without bathroom or other conveniences other than a lavatory on the stair shared by four or six families. Children played in streets or sordid back yards. Yet few complaints were heard, and more wonderful still was the fact that even in such tenements the wife and mother contrived to keep her small home immaculate, her children well dressed and cared for, and the old fashioned range spotless. In East End or West End the character and atmosphere are determined by the mother.

More than that, in these older streets there was remarkable friendliness. Neighbours would talk to each other from open windows and quickly discover if help was needed. In summer most ground floor windows would be open with the housewife leaning out so that I could almost pay some of my pastoral visits on the pavement without going indoors. Mothers could keep an eye on children. The tower blocks of recent years have solved some social problems but created others.

Something of the homeliness and friendliness of the older tenements, with their sense of community, has been lost.

Paternalism is condemned today, but in those days there were still institutions and customs reminiscent of this Victorian quality. One such was the annual New Year's Day Dinner of the Old Man's and Old Woman's Home in Rottenrow. Fifty old men and fifty old ladies assembled in the dining room at two long separate tables. Each woman wore a white shawl and a little cap of lace and velvet. At the end of the room on a dais sat the Lord Provost, the Dean of Guild, the Deacon Convener, the minister of Glasgow, the governors of the Home, and their wives, looking down with interest but not sharing in the dinner. After a bowl of soup had been served, one or two of the governers would carve the turkeys and joints of meat, and afterwards a tot of whisky was distributed all round. After plum pudding, songs and speeches followed. It was a truly Victorian occasion, but one immensely enjoyed.

A continuing task was the conduct of the Cathedral services. The great organ was placed on top of the pulpitum and there was an excellent choir including about twenty boys as well as men and women. Clifford Smith, the brilliant young organist, was an enthusiast constantly adding new works to the music library so that every act of worship was enriched by a wide diversity.

Although from time to time service books have been drawn up and used in the Church of Scotland, no book is obligatory and there has always been a tradition of extempore prayer. This lays a heavy responsibility upon the minister but gives him freedom. If he is wise, he will draw upon the liturgical heritage of the whole Catholic Church and of all the centuries. In my view, the ideal is a combination of liturgical prayer and free prayer or prayers specially prepared for the particular occasion. There has recently been discussion about the language of prayer and a tendency to aim at greater homeliness and simplicity. If this makes for an increased sense of reality in worship it is to be welcomed. In addressing God, Who is not only the great Father in Heaven but also the Maker of all things, visible and invisible, it is essential that we should remember also His majesty and His graciousness. These two must both be reflected in our prayers, and if either the note of the transcendent or the note of simple trust is missing, then something vital has been lost. In corporate worship there should always be a combination of dignity and homeliness. This, at least, was my ideal for our Cathedral Church in Glasgow.

I inherited and continued a very good tradition for the main Sunday morning service, with a metrical psalm, a prose psalm, one of the ancient canticles, an anthem, and the Creed, and a carefully prepared sermon. I restored a more liturgical form of evening service, with a shorter and simpler sermon given much earlier in the service, and the *Nunc Dimittis* sung at the very end after the blessing. In addition to the two great traditional celebrations of holy communion we had a celebration at all the chief festivals as the main service of the day. And on the first Sunday of each month there was a shorter celebration in one of the chapels.

In addition there were many extra acts of worship of different kinds. There was the annual kirkling of the lord provost, magistrates, and councillors, held on the first Sunday after the municipal elections. There was the annual service for the Trades House of Glasgow attended by members of the fourteen ancient guilds or crafts on the first Sunday after the election of the new deacon convener. There were annual services for the Association of Foreman Engineers, for the Masonic Lodge of St John, for the boys of Glasgow Academy, for the pupils of Hutcheson's Grammar School for Girls, for Dennistoun Rotary Club, for the Royal College of Nursing, for the Royal Faculty of Procurators, and many others. There was a special afternoon service on Remembrance Day for members of the Cameronian Regiment. And on innumerable occasions of celebration or sorrow people would come in great numbers.

I mention such services because it seems to me that it is possibly along this kind of line that the Church may best be able to make its appeal heard and its influence felt in coming days. Fewer and fewer, especially of the younger generation, are inclined to make a rule of coming to church on Sundays week by week. It is in any case wrong to make regular attendance at church the chief criterion of Christian life and character, as we have sometimes been tempted to do in the past. We need to be less rigid in our rules and our judgements. There are in the community people at many different stages of the Christian life. They have to discover their own spiritual needs and make their own religious rules; and it is the responsibility of the Church to provide opportunities for them and to help them in their spiritual journeying. Acts of worship on special occasions can provide this. I think for example of a disastrous fire in a city warehouse. Seven young women lost their lives and a wave of horror and sorrow swept across the city. A service was held in the Cathedral on the following day and although the notice was so short the great church was filled from end to end with a deeply reverent congregation. Another such was the death of the much loved Harry Lauder, when we held a service of thanksgiving for all the laughter and delight he had brought to millions by his songs and his inimitable personality. The response was remarkable; and in the congregation there were many who were certainly not regular church goers, but who welcomed the chance of joining in an act of special corporate worship.

Two other rather different kinds of service may be mentioned. One was the three hours devotion on Good Friday. It has no popular appeal but is an opportunity for those so minded to step aside from the activities of daily life and meditate on the great drama of the crucifixion and its meaning. It is held from noon till three o'clock, and is usually divided into seven parts. In each is a hymn, a reading, a prayer, and an address on one of the Words spoken by our Lord from the cross, with intervals of silent prayer. Worshippers come and go, some for only twenty minutes, some for the whole three hours. At first the numbers were small but through the years they increased, and I feel thankful that my successor has carefully carried it on.

Soon after going to Glasgow I proposed a midnight carol service on Christmas Eve. Difficulties were raised. No trams or buses would be running and few would venture to cross the east end of the city at such an hour. But, with its customary generosity, the session gave me permission. I had to ask for voluntary help from the choir but when the evening came there was a reasonably good choir in the organ loft. A great Christmas tree with its lights stood in the nave. Gradually a large congregation assembled who joined with obvious happiness in the familiar carols. An offering was announced. Only then did I realise that no elders were present, but two members of the choir, seeing the situation, quickly came down and undertook the duty. It was a generous offering, and the session was astonished to be told that it had had to be counted in the sacristy by the minister, the beadle, and the doorkeeper. From that day it became a yearly event, supported by all the elders and ever increasing congregations. Eventually many attending had to stand in the nave.

For many generations in Scotland we have been afraid of ritual and symbolism so I will describe what we did. The service began with a processional hymn during which the ministers and choir moved round the whole church, as it were, welcoming everyone, even those in distant corners out of sight of the holy table. The choir then climbed the steps to the organ loft while the clergy went to their stalls in the chancel. After prayers and a reading from the Gospels carols were sung, some by the whole congregation and some by the choir. The great Christmas tree was then blessed. About 11.45, when the address began from the pulpit, all lights were turned out except those on the Christmas tree and the pulpit. At about two minutes to twelve the sermon closed and the people were asked to stand for silent dedication. On the first stroke of midnight all the lights were turned on, flooding the church, and the bell rang out in celebration of the wonderful event of the first Christmas morning. After brief prayers of thanksgiving and dedication and a final carol, usually "O come, all ye faithful ", and the blessing, the people dispersed, the ministers shaking hands with everyone at the doors.

It inaugurated in Scotland one of the most popular and best loved services of the year. Our example was followed in a large number of parishes and is, I think, one of the signs of a deep and sometimes only half conscious spirituality among people of all ages. The Christmas story combines profundity and simplicity and the service offers a new sense of the wonder and joy of Christian worship.

Members of our congregation were scattered far and wide across the city and beyond its boundaries. Pastoral visiting involved travelling by car for long distances. Curiously enough, many of those who had furthest to travel were most regular in attendance. Many of the younger clergy argue that pastoral visiting is unnecessary or that the time could be better spent. I cannot agree. A minister can only be helpful to his parishioners if he knows them in their own homes and keeps in touch with members of the family. A sermon carries more influence if behind it is personal understanding and friendship.

A feature of my Glasgow ministry was my relationship with the lord provost and other civic authorities. As the Cathedral was the mother church of the city its minister was the unofficial chaplain to the town council. At the kirking of the council, the lord provost, magistrates, and councillors came to the Cathedral to ask for God's blessing on themselves and on their public services. They came in their official robes and entered in procession. I invariably asked the lord provost and town clerk to read the lessons. This was both a heavy responsibility for the preacher, and a wonderful opportunity to look at the life of the city in the light of God's Word. I was also invited to say the opening prayers at the first meeting of the newly elected Corporation each year, and to lunch on that and numerous other occasions at the City Chambers. Relations with a long succession of lord provosts were the happiest possible as, with their varied gifts, they carried out the demanding duties of their three year period of office. Some were colourful and ebullient, like the late Sir Patrick Dollan and Sir Victor Warren; others quiet like the late Mr John Biggar who characteristically refused a knighthood. Some were excellent and easy speakers; others, at first awkward and hesitating, after a few months became practised orators. All were able men, who gave an astonishingly generous amount of their time to public service and conscientiously contrived, during their time of office, to rise above party and political controversy.

In 1936 I received an invitation to visit the United States and discovered for the first time the stimulus of foreign travel. Nothing more vividly enlarges one's mental horizons. On this first crossing of the Atlantic I was fortunate to have the company of an older friend, the Reverend Dr. Adam Burnet of St Cuthbert's, Edinburgh. We both stayed for a time in a pleasant country hotel and had time for walking and talking as well as preparation. Never have I known anyone who made such intensely careful preparation for preaching. He was known for the elegance and beauty of his English and was one of the most distinguished preachers of our time. He not only took the greatest pains in writing out his sermon in full, but made a point of finishing by Friday evening and then giving the whole of Saturday to committing his two sermons to memory. In the pulpit he spoke with complete freedom and without a manuscript, and yet sacrificed nothing in felicity of style or language. While I admired such perfection, I never attempted to emulate it. I give much time to preparation and wrote out sermons in full, but I like to have my manuscript in front of me for fairly frequent reference.

My engagements were in the Old First Presbyterian Church in Newark, New Jersey and in Fifth Avenue Presbyterian Church in New York. It was July and extremely hot, and to a Scottish minister it was at first disconcerting to notice that all the worshippers except himself had straw fans, and that the sermon was accompanied by the gentle waving of a thousand fans without thought of irreverence. An American congregation views with disapproval the retiring of a minister to the vestry after the service. He is expected to remain at the chancel steps or in the porch to meet the many people who wait to shake his hand and exchange a few words. It is a sensible and heart warming custom. Later both Adam Burnet and I preached at the huge Conference Centre at Northfield where an annual convention has been held since the time of Moody and Sankey. To me, this was specially interesting because my mother, when young, had been impressed by the preaching of D.L. Moody. The visit did much to widen my outlook and to give me a sense of the Church Universal transcending all frontiers. It prompted me in coming years to invite clergy of other Churches to occupy our pulpit. Among these were Professor Adams Brown of New York, Dr Fosdick of Riverside Baptist Church, Dr B.H. Streeter of Oxford, Canon Anthony Deane of Windsor, Canon J.F. Clayton of Norwich, Dr J.S. Whale of Cheshunt Congregational College, Lord Soper, and many others.

These Glasgow years were crowded with engagements. One was asked to speak at meetings of all kinds, and perhaps too many. Yet it was right that the Church should show interest and give help. There were many invitations to public dinners; on some occasions I had to speak and on others simply to say grace, and it was often a question in my mind as to whether this was a waste of time. I made it a rule, generally speaking, never to introduce the subject of religion to my neighbour at a public dinner, but again and again the subject would be brought up by the man next to me. We had many absorbing conversations on quite deep spiritual questions and I never found the clerical collar any barrier.

I had not yet become greatly involved in the courts and committees of the Church, but I regularly attended our own presbytery in Glasgow and the meeting of the Assembly in May. At that time the outstanding leader was the Very Reverend Dr John White, a man of commanding personality and pungent speech. Proceedings were formal. No minister would think of sitting in the Assembly without a clerical collar and on the opening day or when presenting a report it was almost *de rigeur* to wear a clerical long coat and, out of doors, a top hat. The Sovereign was always represented by the Lord High Commissioner, who was in residence at Holyroodhouse for the ten days of the Assembly. For part of each day he sat in the throne gallery and during the week he and his wife entertained generously at the Palace. At the beginning and at the close, he addressed the Assembly as a distinguished observer on behalf of the Sovereign and without authority over proceedings. This symbolised in a unique way the relationship of Church and State in Scotland.

1937 was for me a year of special interest because my cousin, Lord Kinnaird, was appointed by the King as Lord High Commissioner, and he and his wife were in residence at Holyrood. I stayed as a guest for two days and was also invited to various functions. The ceremonial side was looked after, with characteristic perfection, by the experienced Purse-Bearer, Sir Edward Stevenson. But he could unbend, and in the late evening when their Graces had retired to bed and protocol could be forgotten much fun was had in the equerries' room.

5

A World at War

Already a dark shadow was creeping across Western Europe. Under the ever rising tide of totalitarianism in Germany ominous things were happening. The ruthless persecution of the Jews shocked public opinion. In Glasgow I presided at a large meeting of protest, called to express the horror felt. There were several distinguished speakers, but the speech which impressed me most and seemed the most Christian utterance was that made by a Jew, Victor Gollancz.Things moved to a crisis with the German occupation of Austria, the inexcusable attack on Czechoslovakia, and the invasion of Poland. It had become plain that resistance must be made against power used with such unscrupulous ferocity and on 3 September 1939 the announcement of war brought almost a sense of relief.

Except for younger men in the Forces life went on without much change for several months. That curious time of waiting before the storm broke was unnatural and in some ways demoralising. Restlessness and insecurity were in the air and the sense of impending danger. As the months passed I became increasingly restless and conscious that I must make a difficult choice. On the one hand, I could remain at my post in Glasgow. The clergy were exempt from military service, and in any case I was over the age acceptable at that time. And there were duties at home. On the other hand, I felt a growing discomfort at seeing men day by day preparing for war while not offering to take some share. In the spring of 1940, as events worsened on the Continent, my mind became clear, and I offered myself as a chaplain to the Forces. I had just reached forty and to my chagrin was informed that I was just too old. This made me more determined. I went to London to see the Chaplain General and other authorities and was able to persuade them to accept me, if possible to serve with some Scottish regiment.

On 9 April 1940 the Germans invaded Norway and Denmark. In May there came the evacuation from Dunkirk, but while the last British troops were leaving the beaches it was decided to send an advance guard of a second British Expeditionary Force "to stand alongside the retreating French armies and save a foothold for the allies in Europe" until the time came when the Dunkirk divisions, re-equipped, could be sent overseas again. The 4th and 5th Battalions of the King's Own Scottish Borderers were ordered to take part, and were urgently prepared to go overseas. At this moment I got instructions to join the 5th as their chaplain and to report at Kingsclere near Newbury. On arrival I was welcomed by the Commanding Officer, Lt. Colonel K.A.T. McLennan. It was late afternoon, and they were just starting out on an exercise on the Downs. The Colonel said to me, "Now, Padre, do you like to stay here in the Mess or go out with them in a Bren-gun carrier?" Of course I had no hesitation. It turned out to be a rough but exhilarating ride under a clear windy sky. My only regret was to find on finally dismounting that I had torn my brand new waterproof in many places.

Orders came for the move overseas and on 12 June the 155th Infantry Brigade, consisting of the 7th/9th Royal Scots and the 4th and 5th King's Own Scottish Borderers sailed from Southampton for France. We disembarked at St. Malo and marched immediately to a camp at Cancale six miles away. There we heard of the disastrous fate of the 51st Scottish Highland Division at St. Valery. After a train journey to Silde le Guillaume there was a long hot march to Donfort Foret, all carrying our full load of kit. In the woods there, we recovered our transport, had a good meal, and managed to get some sleep.

The next two days were a time of waiting and uncertainty. None of us except one or two senior officers knew what was likely to happen or how long the new Expeditionary Force would be able to hold its ground. The sound of gun fire periodically filled the air and enemy planes were often overhead. On the Sunday morning I made it known among the scattered groups that I would hold a celebration of holy communion in the open air in a small orchard close by. A large number of men came. A rough trestle table, covered with a linen cloth, formed the holy table. Enemy troops were at best only a few miles away; fighting was imminent; for some of those present death might not be far off. I was the only minister of religion present. I decided to invite any who wished, whether Church of Scotland, Church of England, or Roman Catholic, to receive the sacrament. The great majority did so. There was a wonderful atmosphere of quietness, reverence, and peace. Some weeks later at a chaplain's conference at Cambridge I was challenged by a Jesuit chaplain who sternly informed me that I had broken King's Regulations in holding such an act of worship. My answer was simply that there are times when there are higher values at stake than even loyalty to any rules, and that in similar circumstances I should not hesitate to act again as I had done. Fortunately since then the ecumenical climate has changed and there is understanding and charity among those of diverse traditions.

Soon after it was learned that the British Forces were to be withdrawn and to be evacuated from Cherbourg. Our battalion, the 5th King's Own Scottish Borderers, was to form a rearguard, allowing other units of the Division to pass through. We had moved forward and were now near the village of Volognes, only some fifteen miles from the coast. Directly after early breakfast in a farmhouse kitchen the Colonel said to me, "Padre, could you possibly try to get through to Cherbourg in your car and find out how things are going?" Provided only with a large scale map of the countryside I immediately set off. According to my map there were three roads into Cherbourg. The first was impossible because the French had blown up a bridge to arrest any German advance. On another road, I was informed, German troops were already moving fast. Only one feasible road remained, which I and my driver took.

On reaching the headquarters of "Norman Forces", I at once asked to see the Army Commander, Major-General Marshall-Cornwall and, after considerable argument with some members of his staff, was taken into his room. There I ventured to say to him that our rearguard 5th battalion was in imminent danger of being cut off if the French were allowed to blow up any bridge on the last road. While I was still in the room he rang up the French commander and explained the position. He then sent one of his staff back with me to order the Battalion to withdraw immediately into Cherbourg. It was in many ways a melancholy journey, the ending of another phase of the war with seemingly little achieved. We were ordered to drive all the vehicles into the harbour. My little chaplain's truck had never run better than that day and I watched with regret as it sank out of sight. Perhaps it was a symbol. But we all felt a sense of relief and satisfaction as we steamed out of Cherbourg in the small crowded pleasure steamer, the Manxman, accompanied by a hail of bombs and bullets from enemy planes overhead.

After a short period in Cambridge the Brigade was sent to Norfolk and there we spent that strange summer of 1940. High in the sky, above the sunlit fields the Battle of Britain was being fought by the Royal Air Force. No one except those in the top military circles knew how dangerous the situation was. Every now and again we could see the duels in the air and a plane falling, sometimes in flames, from the sky. Meantime, the task of the land forces was to resist any possible invasion from the sea, to build again their transport and armaments, and undergo rigorous training.

Norfolk is a beautiful county with its woods and fields and small attractive villages, and while keeping in touch with scattered units and visiting men in hospital I was able to see much of the countryside. At the time I was living with the headquarters of the 5th Battalion in the manor house of a very small village, Cockley Clay. On Sunday mornings we had a service in the little parish church, lent to us by the vicar. Directly afterwards I drove to Oxborough to take another service for the 4th Battalion. There the church was spacious and dignified, the Commanding Officer, Colonel Jack Hankey, laid great stress on church parade and expected every available officer and man to turn out. The pipe band marched at the head as the villagers stood at their doors to watch and listen. The Colonel and one of the other officers read the lessons. The church was filled and it was an inspiring sight to look down from the pulpit on such a congregation. Five hundred men's voices singing the Scottish metrical psalms roused from their slumbers the bats that inhabited the church and during my sermon I had to wave them off as they circled round my head. Colonel Hankey was a splendid churchman. He was also the finest regimental officer it has been my good fortune to meet. As one walked with him round the camp it was obvious that he not only knew every man individually but knew and talked about the man's wife and family. And on Sunday afternoons when almost everyone else was resting or playing, he would visit any men in hospital.

In spite of hard training the weeks glided pleasantly by. Local clergy were friendly and I was invited to preach in the fine old parish church of Swaffham at the Harvest Festival. I was also able to drive over to Norwich to see my old friend, Canon John F. Clayton. A delightful feature of the landscape was the unusual number of small mediaeval churches, some with quaint three-decker pulpits, and many with carved screens and pew ends. On the other hand route marches through the flat countryside seemed dull to men accustomed to the hills of Scotland.

In the late autumn orders came to move north, and on the last day of October we left Swaffham in three special trains, reaching Kirkintilloch at noon next day. The people of the little town were marvellously welcoming and although the Battalion was only there for a short time there was great regret that we were to move again shortly. On Sunday 10 November, after church parades in Kilsyth and Kirkintilloch I was able to drive to Glasgow in time to preach at the annual Cameronians' service in the Cathedral. On Sunday 24 November I preached again in the Cathedral at the kirking of the lord provost and magistrates. Next day, with full kit, we left Kirkintilloch at 5.30 a.m. marching through Kilsyth and Stirling to Alloa, arriving at 5.30 p.m.

My house in Glasgow stood empty as the maids found temporary work elsewhere. Having moved the best of my pictures and furniture into store I let the house to the American Ambulance Association and so felt more free and more fully committed to the 52nd Division.

In mid December we moved again to East Lothian. We had companies in North Berwick, Dunbar, and Hedderwick Hill, while I lived at Battalion Headquarters at Tyninghame House. Duties as chaplain kept me fully occupied, conducting at least three and often four church parades in different places and keeping in touch with scattered units. For the men, life was inevitably monotonous but their behaviour in leisure seemed remarkably good. Of course there was occasional delinquency. One day after lunch about twenty men passed the window doing punishment drill. The adjutant said, "Padre, I expect you noticed that about three-quarters of those were, as usual, your Glasgow parishioners." "Yes," I said, "but if we were on active service and in a tight corner I would sooner have some of those chaps around me than most of the others."

Once again the Division moved, and this time to Perthshire and I was billeted in Callander. Though far from their native Dumfriesshire and Wigtownshire, the majority of the Borderers were countrymen and used to country ways. A large contingent of Lancashire men had been drafted in and though they spoke a different dialect seemed to assimilate contentedly. I usually conducted a parade service in St. Kessog's and often two or three services for other units. Everyone liked to be free in the afternoon so I had to have all the services over by lunch time. This meant fast driving and short sermons. Apart from this I gave talks on current affairs, ran a National Savings Scheme, helped to supply "comforts" and visited men in hospital. I took part in exercises and route marches and went to weekly dances though I cannot dance myself. One came to know men individually and they all knew that I was accessible. Comradeship in a regiment is a wonderful thing, and was especially so when men were recruited locally and had strong ties of tradition and a common love of the same fields and hills. In all my work I had the sympathetic support of the commanding officers. One could count on them setting a good example at church parade.

Since then church parades have become voluntary. Theoretically, it seems at first sight that any compulsion in religion is wrong except in the case of young children. You cannot make a man a Christian against his will. On the other hand in the army a man's life is regulated by a more thorough discipline than in civilian life. This curtailment of freedom is generally accepted by the serving soldier. He is part of a corporate unit which demands a loyalty that gives strength and confidence. As a member of his regiment he often does things he might not have chosen but which he accepts. For some men church parade would come into this category.

Ours is a Christian country; and that has always been recognised in the Forces. Many regiments have a religious motto. The badge of the King's Own Scottish Borderers includes the motto, *"Nisi Dominus Frustra"*. It is natural therefore that in the week by week programme of an army unit attendance at church should be included. If a man has scruples of conscience he can be excused but, to the best of my limited experience, church parade was never seriously resented. To make it purely voluntary is to change the whole conception. Under this, moral courage of an unusual quality is demanded from young men, many of them incapable of making a Christian witness even if they secretly like to do it. Church parade brought men within the sound of the Christian Gospel. It gave them the experience of prayer and worship. To any who were troubled, it gave the offer of comfort and strength. To some who were careless or cynical it might give a glimpse of spiritual realities. To the chaplain, it was a frightening but wonderful opportunity. And from time to time the results could be seen in a regimental confirmation service at which twenty or thirty young men would courageously profess their faith in public.

After some months we moved northwards to Banffshire. To me the change was welcome. We were close to the sea on a rugged stretch of coast and I loved the long views and the great skyscapes. For the first few months I lived once again with the 5th Battalion in Banff, an unspoilt country town with old houses and streets of character. Our mess was a large house on the edge of the cliffs looking across the bay to Macduff. There, on the lawn in the open air at 7.15 every morning the officers were given P.T. exercises by a stern and energetic sergeant. On winter days the great sea rollers surged on the beach below. It was formidable to come straight from bed into the icy wind, but the sergeant made certain that we didn't feel the cold for long.

Monotony was the chief enemy. I had good relations with the Transport Sergeant and acquired the use of a large Norton motor cycle, which I enjoyed, and which allowed me to get the feel of the countryside better than in my truck. A notice appeared in Battalion Orders one day that all officers in the 5th Battalion would undergo a motor cycle test. The course took us over narrow tracks and steep gradients and one of the worst hazards was a large pool of thick mud. To my un-Christian delight, as I reached it I saw the second-in-command completely immobilised in the mud. He was a heavy and rather indolent man. A sergeant and a corporal were struggling to extricate him, and not even the passing of the chaplain modified the stream of invective.

From time to time chaplains met to compare notes. I especially enjoyed such meetings with John Fraser, Senior Chaplain to the Division, Willie Tyndall, who was with a regiment of Royal Artillery, and Ronald Selby Wright who was attached to the Royal Scots. We would meet at some country inn, have lunch, and then an afternoon of talk. A padre has a unique position. Officers, N.C.O.s, and men alike are his parishioners and have an equal claim on him. He is never certain how far his pastoral and spiritual endeavours are effective, but success in spiritual things can never be measured. Men serving their country should know that the Church stands by them and is ready to give support. In June 1942 I suggested that we should hold a conference and retreat for all chaplains in the Division. John Fraser readily agreed, leaving the arrangements to me. It was held some weeks later and gave us the opportunity of meeting in prayer and at holy communion and of exchanging views on our task.

The second part of my stay in the North was spent with the 4th Battalion at Buckie, a few miles along the coast. My windows looked out on its harbour. Several boats had succeeded in escaping from Norway, some scarred with bomb or bullet marks. In Buckie they found themselves in a community like their own and were soon at home. The council allocated part of the harbour to them and it was good to see the two fleets moving out in friendly understanding. Several Norwegian men married Buckie girls.

Perhaps the best picture of this restless ministry can be given by extracts from a diary. "Thursday, 16 April. P.T. at 7.15 a.m. 'O Group' conference at the orderly room after breakfast. Then wrote until 12. Drove southwards towards Turriff and visited three different isolated units of R.A.S.C. men. Called at the tiny schoolhouse near two of them and arranged to open a library two nights a week for the troops. My driver Hewit and I ate our rations in a field looking towards the Grampians. Back to Banff, where the Senior Chaplain, John Fraser, came to see me about various things. He stayed to tea. More writing after dinner. Then Jim Henderson (a Company Commander) and I called at the manse. Talked and played bridge."

"Sunday 21 June. Church parade at 10 a.m. Celebration of holy communion with three officers and three N.C.O.s from each Company as elders. Over a hundred took communion. Drove to Botriphnie to take Church Parade for the Reconnaissance Regiment in the little parish church. Marched back afterwards with Colonel Hankey and the troops. Lunched in the mess. Long talk with Haddersley, C. of E. chaplain, in the garden. Tea at the manse at Keith. Then north to Spey Bay to take an evening service for an Anti-Aircraft Battery. All Londoners, so took shortened Evensong. Talked to the men afterwards, and then had supper with the Battery Commander, and discussed many things.."

In the spring of that year, 1942, I was once again confronted by a very difficult decision. When I left Glasgow to join the Chaplain's Department I had made what seemed in the circumstances adequate arrangements for carrying on the day to day duties at the Cathedral. A very senior minister, the Very Reverend Dr P.D. Thomson, kindly agreed to keep general oversight, and the two assistant ministers, James Bulloch and William Syme, both able and conscientious men, were to be in charge of the services and the pastoral work. But they were both young and the strain must have been heavy, and in the early spring of 1942 James Bulloch had a serious breakdown in health. Dr P.D. Thomson and the session clerk, Robert Cullen, asked to see me; and after a long discussion appealed to me to apply for release from the army. It was an unexpected situation. After further talks with Dr John White and the presbytery clerk, my duty seemed clear. I could not allow James Bulloch to further endanger his health. More than that, the Cathedral was the mother church of the great city; the war had reached an anxious stage; spiritual leadership and support were needed, and it was pointed out to me that I could be of more use at my responsible post in Glasgow than anywhere else. I could not resist these arguments. And a congregational meeting at the Cathedral strongly supported a petition to the War Office for my release. It was with very mixed feelings that I looked forward to the future, and above all with deep regret at the thought of leaving the many in the 52nd Division to whom I had become so attached

I returned to Banffshire for some time. My diary records, "Sunday 28 June. Took my last Church Parade service in the big parish church at 11. A splendid turn out of the Battalion and the ordinary congregation. Preached on the K.O.S.B. motto: *Nisi Dominus Frustra.*" "Monday 29 June. To the mess where the officers gave a farewell dinner for me. The C.O., Colonel T. Murray, made a charming speech, and I was presented with a beautiful silver salver. Felt almost overwhelmed; everyone marvellously kind and friendly. Very sad saying goodbye."

There seemed no likelihood of the Division being called to overseas service again for a long time. Instead they devoted the next two years to intensive training in mountain warfare. As George Blake wrote in his book, *Mountain and Flood,* "The adventures of the 52nd (Lowland) Division in the War of 1939-1945 form a story as strange as any in the annals of the British Army. It is certain that no other major formation underwent such a long, arduous and varied period of training, was so long denied the opportunity of proving itself in action, or went into major battle finally in such unforeseen circumstances ..... In the event, the Division did not go into action until late October 1944; and then the lads who wore on their sleeves the proud "Mountain" legend of their specialised training, were led to assault the low beaches and dykes of South Beveland-Walcheren and, in the conquest of these Dutch islands, to fight largely under sea level and often to move in boats." At the end of the War, although I had been for so long only on the "home front", the King's Own Scottish Borderers made me an honorary member of the Regiment, an honour I value more than words can say.

The Glasgow to which I returned was different from the city I left in 1940. In a very real sense the whole community was geared to war conditions. My house being let, I had to look for somewhere to live and was fortunate to find a small flat in St Vincent Street in the centre of the city. After some painting I had a little furniture and a few pictures installed, and my faithful cook, Flora Cant, came back at once. My first care was the Cathedral and its services, and the members of our congregation. Owing to the blackout, evening services had been given up and an afternoon service instituted. We also had a short morning service at 10 a.m. When enemy bombers appeared over Glasgow I usually spent the night at the Royal Infirmary. We had two watchmen on duty at the Cathedral. On one night fire bombs landed on the roof but were quickly extinguished. I myself enrolled in a fire watching group. Service men on leave often found it difficult to get accommodation at short notice and I was able to get permission from the Ministry of Works to use our crypt as a night shelter in case of need.

We had many special acts of worship. Thursday 2 September was declared ''A Day of National Prayer and Dedication'' and evoked a wide response. We had a service at 10.30 a.m. led by representatives of all the different denominations, followed by a celebration of holy communion. In the afternoon there was a service for the Forces; and at 7.30 p.m. a great civic service attended by the lord provost and magistrates, the Merchants' House, the Trades House, and many other public bodies. On Sunday, 1 November, we had a parade service for 500 W.R.N.S., A.T.S. and W.A.A.F. Another moving act of worship was a service of intercession for the Channel Islands then occupied by German troops. 400 refugees from the Islands attended. Many Norwegians were in Glasgow and on 17 May, Norway's National Day, we lent the Cathedral for a service conducted by their chaplain, Pastor Brunwand. Such prayer means a public acknowledgement of our dependence on God.

In wartime the Christian scale of values is forgotten or blurred. In a good many sermons I tried to commend the gentler virtues of forgiveness, pity, and humility. There was a demand for reprisals when it was said that Germans were ill-treating prisoners of war and I made an urgent plea that we should resist such a temptation. Later in the strain of war things were done which brought discredit on our country. I became a member of the Huts and Canteens Committee under Dr Charles Warr. In these canteens serving men and women could find not only supplies but also personal understanding and friendship. At a different level I became a member of the Assembly Commission under Professor John Baillie ''to interpret the Will of God for our Time.'' It was to take a large view from the Christian angle; to analyse the cause of our failures; and to suggest urgent changes in the structure of the Church and the life of the nations. I myself was made convener of a sub-committee on The Reconstruction of the International Order, consisting of Sir James Dunnett, Dr George MacLeod, and Professor Gervase Riddell. The whole Report, when presented by John Baillie, drew much interest both north and south of the Border.

Despite the demands of war a number of social activities continued on a small scale. Among these was a dinner party given by Sir Steven Bilsland in honour of Mr Anthony Eden. It was a mixed company, men only, and included Sir Stephen Piggott, Chairman of John Brown's, Sir Harold

Yarrow, Sir Maurice Denny, all outstanding men in shipbuilding, Sir Robert Bruce, Editor of *The Glasgow Herald,* and the American film star, Edward G. Robinson. In the autumn, an event that gave me great happiness was the holding of a confirmation school for men of the 9th Armoured Division. It was organised by one of the most brilliant of the younger chaplains, the Reverend Ian Macaulay, and held at Belsay Castle in Northumberland. About 270 Church of England and 70 Church of Scotland men were present and a downstairs room had been converted into a chapel. Prayers at 8.15 were followed by breakfast with a lecture and discussion at 10 a.m. The afternoons were free. At 5 p.m. we had prayers with a lecture and discussion before supper at 7.30 and an evening act of worship at 10 p.m. Ian had asked me to give six lectures on the Church, her faith and sacraments, prayer and the Christian life. Only a few months later Ian Macaulay went overseas and was killed in action.

In late July 1943 an event took place quite unexpectedly, as such things do, which changed my life. As one of the Trustees of Iona Abbey I had occasion to visit it with James Richardson, H.M. Inspector of Ancient Monuments, and Ian Lindsay, the consultant architect. We travelled by train to Oban where we joined the Mull steamer. After being rowed ashore at Craignure we continued in a hired car through Glen More and along the Ross of Mull while others made the journey in the mail bus. As we were preparing to go down to the Iona Ferry, I noticed a charming, quiet, and reserved girl about to carry her luggage. Prompted by more than good manners, I asked if I might carry her large suitcase. When we reached the island, among those on the jetty I recognised Sir David Russell, who invited me to lunch next day. Then, to my surprise, I saw that he escorted our travelling companion up the hill. Next day I met Peggy Martin, as her name turned out to be, and we found we had much to talk about. During the next forty-eight hours I combined business with pleasure. Sir David and Lady Russell were kind and understanding; Jamie Richardson and George MacLeod were tactful. Later on they asserted that my concern with plans for the Abbey was less than it might have been. This sudden and all too short friendship continued and was followed by an invitation from Mrs. Martin to stay for a weekend at Yately in Berkshire where Peggy and she were living. After that I had no doubt that I had found the one person who, above all others, could give me the happiness of a perfect companionship for life.

Our wedding took place in the Cathedral on 19 January. The great church was crowded from end to end. As her father was on active service in India the bride was given away by her brother, Major Peter Martin, The 22nd (Cheshire) Regiment. The Very Reverend Charles Warr, Archdeacon A.O.N. Lee, and Professor Donald Baillie officiated and the best man was Dr George MacLeod. It was the supreme day of my life. Until then I had never had much time to think of marriage, for life was too full and the days too crowded. But something was missing. After that first meeting in Iona and since our wedding day I discovered that life had taken on a new dimension.

We spent our fortnight's holiday in Skye. Though by the calendar it was "the dead of winter", we had one of those spells of mild weather and brilliant sunshine sometimes found in the islands even at that time. We had the little old hotel at Kyleakin entirely to ourselves. Shrubs and flowers were budding. The mountains stood up clear and magnificent against a cloudless sky, their summits were crowned with snow. Everywhere the ground was carpeted with snowdrops. After a week we went on to Dunvegan to lunch with that great lady, Dame Flora MacLeod, and then to Portree. We had no car, but had many walks across the moor or along the shore. War belonged to another planet.

And then duty called us to war-time Glasgow. It was not easy for my wife to make her home in the great rumbustious city. Most of her associations were with the army, and especially with India. Her father, Colonel C. de C. Martin, was in the Indian Medical Service; her grandfather, General Sir Malcolm Grover, had been G.O.C. Quetta Division; and many older relations had risen high in the Indian Civil Service. She had spent the last few years with her parents in Burma, only returning shortly before the outbreak of war. Now she had to adjust to life as a clergyman's wife in a large, noisy city. We decided to stay on meanwhile in my small flat in St Vincent Street, which was central and convenient for buses and trams, and there we remained until the end of the war.

6

Cathedral Heritage

I had not been long at the Cathedral before I saw how much needed to be done to restore the interior. On the whole the structure of the great church had been well preserved. After the reformation it was under the care of the town council. As time passed and the population of the town increased it became a collegiate charge with two ministers. A new congregation to serve the landward part of the parish was formed in 1595 with the name of the Barony of Glasgow and worshipped in the lower church or crypt. Later still, in 1647, a third congregation was formed and worshipped in the nave under the name of the Outer High Church. A dividing wall was built and galleries erected. For about two hundred and fifty years this strange arrangement continued with three congregations under one roof as at St Mary's Dundee and St Nicholas in Aberdeen. In 1800 the Barony erected a church of its own and in 1836 the Outer High Church built St Paul's nearer the city centre. It was only in 1849, after some three hundred years, that the care of the Cathedral was put on a new footing. A deed was executed by the Commissioners of Woods and Forests, setting out that "the Cathedral of Glasgow, the property of Her Majesty, has recently been repaired and restored, and that the Lord Provost, Magistrates and Council of the City of Glasgow, as representing the community thereof, have requested that we should place the custody and care of the said building with them, in order to ensure the due protection and care and preservation thereof; with which request we have resolved to comply." In other words, the Cathedral became the property of the Crown and its structural maintenance became the reponsibility of the Office of Public Works.

Some solution of this kind may prove necessary elsewhere. It has obvious advantages and possible disadvantages. A venerable and historic place of worship will not be allowed to deteriorate. On the other hand, there is the risk that a place of worship may no longer be under the proper control and jurisdiction of the ecclesiastical authorities. The only solution lies in harmonious relations between the church authorities and government department concerned. During my thirty years in Glasgow we had such a relationship and there was never tension. A block grant was set aside by the Department each year to be spent on the fabric. The officials with whom we were mostly in contact were the Director of the Office of Works in Edinburgh and the senior architect and, for consultation, the Inspector of Ancient Monuments for Scotland. I should like to express my deep appreciation of the kindness and consideration shewn us by Wilson Paterson, H.G. White, and Stewart Cruden.

We were always informed of any proposed structural repairs and improvement before they were undertaken. More than that, in any year when necessary repairs had not used all the money available, the senior architect of the Office of Works would ask if there was any project or improvement that I would care to suggest. Under the present arrangement, while the structure of the Cathedral as a whole is under the control of the government department, the furnishings of the church are the property of the minister and kirk session; and it is they who have the continuous use of the church for divine service and religious gatherings of all kinds. What is of vital importance is that a cathedral church should never be thought of simply as a magnificent monument but always as a living centre of worship, prayer, and spiritual life.

When I first came to the city as minister of Glasgow I realised that I was entering into a long and splendid heritage. The Cathedral is the greatest mediaeval place of worship still in use in Scotland, both in size and in splendour; but soon I felt that there were certain things needing to be done to restore it to something more of its former beauty and its former wideness of use. One of these things was the installation of fine stained glass. Not a single scrap of mediaeval glass has survived. Between 1856 and 1864 no fewer than 82 windows had been filled, by public subscription, with painted glass made in Munich and Dresden. At the time it was considered the best obtainable, but the standard of art and craftsmanship in that period was extremely mediocre. These German windows let in little light and gave a sense of gloom to the whole church, and many were in poor condition with the paint fading or flaking off. Another project was to bring the whole of the great church into use. Only the choir was furnished, crowded with large oak pews up to the east wall. There was no seating in the nave, though chairs could be brought in for special occasions. The wonderful crypt with the tomb of St Mungo, the chapter house, the east chapels, and the Blacader Aisle were all unfurnished and unlit. I longed to see the great church restored to use in all its parts.

In conversation I soon discovered that there would be strong support for such ideas. Paying a call one afternoon on a devoted member, Mrs. Donaldson of the well known shipping line, to whom I had previously confided some of my ideas, as I was saying goodbye an envelope was put in my hand. "I have been laying a pound or two aside," she said, "to help with your plans for the Cathedral. You are to spend it on whatever you like and it is not to go through any committees." When I got home and opened the envelope it contained £1,000 in notes, a large sum in those days. I soon decided I would use it for the proper lighting of the crypt and the Blacader Aisle. The architect, Mr Wilson Paterson, prepared a design for tall wrought iron lamps which would throw light not only downwards but upwards on to the stone vaulting. It was possible, with the generous gift, to place eight splendid lamps in the lower church and four in the Blacader Aisle, revealing the beauties of the stonework as it had never before been seen even in the thirteenth and fifteenth centuries.

In the spring of 1936 I first met two distinguished men who were to give me encouragement and help in the work of restoration and whose friendship enriched all my subsequent years in Glasgow. One was Sir John Stirling-Maxwell of Pollok; a great landowner, a lover of the arts, and a generous citizen of Glasgow with wide ranging knowledge both of antiquarian history of forestry, botany, and natural history. His house, now presented to the city, was full of beautiful pictures, furniture, and china where it was a joy to spend even a few hours of conversation. The other was Sir Steven Bilsland, later Lord Bilsland, a great industrialist and banker, supporter of many good causes, looked up to by people in all walks of life for integrity of character, wise judgement, and genial humanity.

Among others who gave valued and enthusiastic advice were the distinguished artist, Sir D.Y. Cameron, and Sir Robert Bruce, editor of *The Glasgow Herald.* With their support and that of several others we arranged for a meeting in the Merchants' House. There was a crowded attendance, Sir D.Y. Cameron gave an excellent address in his characteristic elequent and appealing manner, and a "Society of Friends of Glasgow Cathedral" was brought into being. If the Society was to win and hold confidence it was necessary to make sure that the executive committee contained as representative and as knowledgeable a group of members as possible. Only then could it count on the respect and trust of the kirk session, the Ministry of Works, and the general public. So, in addition to representatives of the kirk session and congregation, it included a representative of the Board of Ancient Monuments, the Senior Architect of the Ministry of Works, Mr. Wilson Paterson, and, as chief external consultant, the distinguished architect, Sir Edward Maufe.

The Cathedral kirk session, satisfied by the competence of this committee, agreed that all future gifts and all proposed plans of improvement should pass through this committee and then be submitted to the session for final approval. It was an arrangement which operated through the following years with remarkable success. Only gifts which commended themselves to a knowledgeable and experienced group of people would be accepted. From the beginning we agreed that for a great and historic place of worship only furnishings and stained glass of the finest quality could be accepted.

I was convinced that when the restoration plans became known many people would wish to offer a gift of some sort, whether large or small. With much thought I prepared a list of possible gifts to suit donors of different financial abilities. Often someone would want to offer a gift as a memorial to a loved member of their family; sometimes in thanksgiving for some blessing or happiness that had come to them. Sometimes it was the gift of an institution, or a school, or a regiment. As the years passed the church was constantly being enriched by presents of all kinds. The family of the late Lord Maclay had the ancient chapter house rehabilitated and furnished with a fine refectory table and a set of magnificent Charles II armchairs. Members of the Royal College of Nursing helped to furnish as a special corner for nurses the tiny chapel of St. Andrew in the lower church. Gifts from individuals were many and varied; a large ornamental clock to hang over the west door in the nave; a prayer desk and lectern for the Blacader Aisle, silver flower bowls for the chancel, a valuable eastern rug for the tomb of St Mungo, a magnificent carved wood eagle lectern of the seventeenth century, an old brass hanging lamp for the chapter house.

When visiting a small antique shop in Stirling, my wife and I came upon an old painting, of obvious quality, depicting the Nativity. We managed to buy it at a very reasonable cost. It was, however, in poor condition, very dark and dirty. I took it to the Art Gallery to shew Dr Tom Honeyman, the Director, who with characteristic kindness agreed to have it cleaned by one of their expert restorers. It was pronounced by an acknowledged authority to be an early seventeenth century Flemish work, and when cleaned was both impressive and religiously appealing. After much thought I decided to have it hung on one of the great piers of the crossing at the east end of the nave, the first picture, I suppose, that has had a place in the Cathedral since the reformation. In this painting the Christ Child is lying on the straw, His mother sitting by Him, Joseph and a group of others standing in the background. A small boy in a red coat is kneeling reverently by the cradle with a large dog beside him. It is evening, but no lamp or candle is shewn. In the foreground, the stable and the faces are lit up by a soft and mysterious glow, the light apparently created by the Christ Child.

There was urgent need for better and fine stained glass and this was a more delicate matter than might at first appear. Most of the glass already installed had originally been given by the heads of many leading families in Scotland. Without consulting the present heads of many of these families, it could not be removed. We realised also that those concerned might wish to preserve in some way their family association. In order to meet these difficulties with courtesy it was decided that I should try to discover the direct descendant of any original donor and write to him explaining our plans and hopes. This I did, writing first to one who I knew would take a wide and generous view, the late Duke of Buccleuch and Queensberry. I explained that we would like to replace his family window by fine contemporary glass, asked if he would be able to bear the expense himself and, if not, whether he would give us permission to find a new donor and artist. In any case we proposed to have his family coat of arms inserted once again. With characteristic sympathy he agreed, saying that while he did not feel able to undertake it himself he had no objection to our finding a donor for a new window. My task was made much easier in approaching others. Some, such as Sir John Stirling-Maxwell and Sir Archibald Campbell of Garscube and Succoth, generously agreed to bear the expense of replacing their family windows. Others willingly accepted our proposal to find new donors.

After careful consideration and viewing of their work we drew up a panel of artists, some Scottish, some English, from whom donors might choose. For a large church, where a good many windows are being fitted with new glass at the same time, it is also desirable to have a carefully thought out plan of subjects. This I prepared for all the windows in the choir and transepts and also for the great west window. It seemed selfish that every window in a cathedral church should be filled with stained glass at the same time. There might well be brilliant artists in a future generation for whose work room should be available. We therefore decided not to accept offers for any new windows in the nave. During the war the whole project had to be suspended but immediately afterwards it was continued. People sometimes suggested that it must have been difficult to find donors for such costly gifts, but it was not so. Actually we had more offers than we could accept. The choice of artists and designs can also be delicate. When a donor offered to present a window, to avoid any misunderstanding we suggested an artist, or allowed the donor to select one from the agreed panel. The artist was then invited to prepare a design, shewing the appropriate subject for that window. He was to be paid a fair price for the design, but with no commitment to use it. If the design seemed suitable and attractive he was asked to make the window; if not, some other artist was approached. In the case of a very important window, such as that above the great west door, two or three different artists were invited to submit designs from which the final choice could be made.

The response was extremely gratifying. The choice of artists and designs may seem complex. It certainly involved a great deal of time, thought, and discussion, and trustful co-operation on the part of the donors, but in furnishing and adorning a place of worship only the best is good enough. In the end, I think, all the donors were satisfied. The new glass brought light and radiance into the old church, and the variety of styles, while not clashing, lends individual interest to every window. The artists who contributed included Francis Spear, Herbert Hendrie, Carl Edwards, Robert Armitage, Sadie Pritchard, Marion Grant, Christopher Webb, William Wilson, Gordon Webster, and Harry Stammers. All our long and sometimes difficult labours were well rewarded when we had a visit from an acknowledged expert, the late Very Reverend Dr Milner White, Dean of York. As he said goodbye, after a careful inspection of the various windows, he said to me, "I expect you know that you now have here in your Cathedral the most comprehensive and representative collection of modern stained glass anywhere in Britain."

A good many of the new windows were given by private individuals, often in memory of their own families. Others were presented by institutions such as the Merchants' House, the Trades House of Glasgow, and the Masonic Lodge of Glasgow St John. The town council presented the magnificent west window depicting the creation. In the south transept the window presented by the four Scottish Divisions was unveiled by Her Majesty the Queen Mother. And in the north transept, windows commemorating the officers and men of the Royal Navy, the R.N.V.R., the Merchant Navy, and the Royal Air Force were unveiled by Her Royal Highness the Princess Margaret. To commemorate the officers and men of the Scots Guards who fell in the two World Wars, His Royal Highness the late Duke of Gloucester unveiled a window at the north end of the west wall. We greatly valued the association which the new windows gave us with many different sections and aspects of the life of the city and the nation.

7

Journeyings in India

In the spring of 1947 I was confronted by an unexpected request. After more than twenty years of negotiation several of the separated branches of the Church in South India had agreed to form a single Church. It was an event of major significance in the Christian world scene and one which would have far reaching ecumenical consequences. Churches in many parts of the world were invited to send delegates to the Service of Inauguration in Madras, and the General Assembly appointed me to represent the Church of Scotland. This was followed by a request from the Foreign Mission Committee, as it was then called, that my wife and I should visit as many as possible of our mission stations all over India. Only a few months previously, independence had been promised to India and Pakistan. The whole sub-continent was restless and confused, and in many parts fighting had broken out between Muslims and Hindus. No one could predict the attitude of the new governments to Christian evangelism and missionaries felt that a question mark hung above their future work and witness. In this context the home Church felt that a visit from Scotland might bring encouragement and cheer. For my wife and myself it meant an absence of several months, but our kirk session acquiesced and allowed me to go with a clear conscience.

Various preparations had to be made for the care of the Cathedral in my absence. I also had talks with the staff of the Overseas Department to make myself familiar with urgent missionary problems and obtain a complete list of all our missionaries working in hospitals, schools, and evangelistic centres. As they were scattered across almost the whole of India it involved a good deal of travelling. Different areas presented different problems, some of them better discussed on the spot than in Edinburgh. Over all hung the question of the unpredictable future relationship between the missions and the new governments. A new chapter in the history of the sub-continent was beginning and the Church must be alert to its implications, the problems and the opportunities.

56

At last preparations were completed and, thanks to the help of our friend, Commodore Sir David Bone, a nice cabin had been secured on the Anchor Line ship *Celicia* of 12,000 tons. On Saturday, 30 August, we steamed out of Liverpool. Several other clergy were on board and with the agreement of the Captain and Purser it was decided to hold worship in the main lounge on Sundays. A small room was allotted to us for brief daily services, and Roman Catholics had their own arrangements for Mass. Among the clergy were an elderly Methodist minister, the Reverend E.W.A. Thomson, a missionary, the Reverend J. Clutterbuck, and the Reverend T. Legg of the London Missionary Society who was to be one of the bishops of the new United Church of South India. Also on board was Mr Sadik, Secretary of the National Christian Council of India, with whom I had much informative conversation. On the first Sunday at sea, my diary records; "Went to a celebration of holy communion at 7.30 a.m. in the Gallery, taken by a young Anglican of the Church Missionary Society. About twenty there. At 11 o'clock, by request of the Purser, I took the ship's service. The First Officer read the Lessons and Hilliard, an Anglican S.P.G. missionary from Chota in Nagpur, took the intercessions. I spoke on 'The Church as the Family of God'. About eighty there. The saloon looked very nice with an altar cloth with cross and flowers." This first Sunday was typical of the ecumenical spirit which transcended differences.

Given good weather, nothing is more restful than a sea voyage. Demands are left behind. Great stretches of sea and sky widen one's mental and physical horizons to give an ampler perspective. I was glad to have time for writing and reading. The vastness and grandeur of sea, sky, wind, and stars draws the little group on the ship closer to one another. At Port Said we went ashore for a few hours, where I had a feeling I had never experienced in any other town, the sensation of evil, indescribable but intensely real. In all large cities there is sordidness, but in Port Said, evil seemed to prevail. It was a terrible reflection. Next day some of us hired a car and drove to Cairo. We rode out on camels to see· the Pyramids and the Sphynx, marvellous in their timelessness. In the largest of the mosques we walked into a huge chamber where many knelt at prayer. My wife whispered to me, "It must be impossible, but I seem to recognise that man prostrated quite near to us." We looked more closely and found it was the driver of our taxi. Could one imagine such a thing in London or New York in a Christian place of worship? The devotion of many Muslims and the unselfconscious practice of their religious duties is remarkable. My diary records how one evening, "As the sun set we watched several Muslims of the crew saying their evening prayers most devoutly, their bowed figures silhouetted against the darkening sky."

As we travelled towards Bombay we heard ominous reports. The Punjab was terribly disturbed, and in Delhi rioting and communal fighting was so serious that troops and police were posted on roof tops all over the city with orders to fire to kill. There were more than 400 casualties in a day. Early on Wednesday, 17 September, we steamed into Bombay; "the great bay full of shipping of all sorts and everything shimmering in the early morning sunlight. Then followed an hour of pandemonium till we had all our luggage ashore and through the customs." We were met by the Reverend Dr James Kellock and his charming vivacious wife and taken straight to Wilson College to spend a few days. It is one of the best of our Missionary Colleges with a most beautiful situation on the shore of the huge bay, not far from Malabar Hill and looking south across the Arabian Sea.

The next few days were crowded, meeting members of staff and students, visiting schools and churches, talking about missionary problems, and preaching in the Scots Church. One's first glimpse of an eastern city was something of a shock; the grotesquely crowded streets, the noise, the smells, and above all the incredible poverty. In a city like Bombay or Calcutta thousands of men, women, and children have no home other than the streets, are largely dependent on charity for their daily food, and have to sleep at night on the pavements, on window sills, or in unlit alleys. No one who has never travelled in the East can even picture it in imagination. In vivid contrast, we lunched one day at Government House. The last British Governor, Sir John Colville, was extremely popular and had been asked to remain in office for a few months after independence had been granted. He was away from home, but we spent some delightful hours with Lady Colville, who was already a friend.

Wherever possible we travelled by train to see the countryside. On 23 September we set off southwards from Bombay. "Passed through most beautiful country between Bombay and Poona, the train climbing slowly up into wooded hills, with deep gullies and waterfalls and every kind of tree and shrub, very luxuriant, like the wilder parts of Perthshire. After Poona the country grew much flatter with many herds of cattle and small paddy fields. We have our meals brought to us in the carriage." Next day: "Travelled through very varied country, sometimes hilly and wooded, sometimes flat and marshy. Herds of buffalo, cows, and goats wherever there was any pasture, and saw one herd of large black boars. The people much darker in skin and the villages more primitive, consisting almost entirely of thatched huts. One especially beautiful place is Pattur, a village in a wide valley, with rugged precipitous mountain ridges on either side. Spent the day looking at the endlessly varied panorama of Indian country life. At Arkonam, the Reverend E.O. Shaw met us and brought the suggested programme for the next three weeks. Reached Madras at 8.40 p.m." There we were the guests of Mr and Mrs J.G. Young.

At 6.45 the next day we breakfasted and caught the train to Tambaram for the last session of the South Indian United Church (Presbyterian and Congregational), where the final resolutions to enter the new Church of South India were made. Then eight of us, representatives of other Churches and Societies, gave short messages of greeting. The Moderator celebrated holy communion and the Assembly dissolved. Peggy and I lunched with Dr Alec Boyd, Principal of the College, then went back to Madras where at St George's Cathedral I presented copies of our Book of Common Order and Ordinal to each of the bishops designate.

Saturday was the day chosen for the service of inauguration of the new Church of South India. As we drove to St George's Cathedral at 7.30 a.m. in brilliant sunlight the streets echoed to the sound of church bells almost as though it had been an English city. When we arrived the large pundal, or annexe, was already filled with 1,800 people and the church practically full. Peggy and I were in the front and so had a magnificent view. I almost melted in the heat in my red cassock and black gown. The service began at 8 a.m. The presiding bishop, an Indian, Bishop Jacob, was extremely impressive and the triumphant singing of the *Te Deum* was superb. After twenty minutes we returned to the church for the consecration of the new bishops. They were robed in white rochet, purple cincture, saffron coloured stole, pectoral cross, no mitre, carried a staff, and numbered fifteen. The consecration was carried out by the laying on of hands by the three former bishops of the Anglican Church, three presbyters of the United Church of South India, and three of the Methodist Church. The Reverend J. Hooper preached an excellent sermon and holy communion followed. Never have I felt more conscious of the power of the Holy Spirit than that morning. As we emerged into the streets at 12.30 old labels had been discarded and a new inclusive Christian community had come into being.

That evening a large public meeting, attended by about 2,000 was held in the open air in the compound of Meston College. Many messages were read and addresses given by the Honourable T. Thomas, representing the Government, by Dr Thomson of the U.S.A., the Reverend E.W. Ronson, and myself. Darkness fell but the speaking continued and the great audience was loath to disperse. On the following day, Sunday, visitors preached in Madras churches. "We drove to St George's Cathedral for the sung eucharist at 8.15 a.m., at which I preached," says my diary. "At 12 I went to lunch at the Women's Christian College where all the bishops are staying. Had a good deal of conversation with Bishop Hollis, Bishop Lesslie Newbiggin, Bishop Packenham Walsh, and others, and also with the Principal, Miss Brockway, and the Vice-Principal, Miss George. We had Indian food." At 6 p.m. I preached at St Matthias Church on the function of the Church in the world to a large congregation. We had magnificent singing, much ceremonial, and incense. Afterwards we dined with the session clerk of the Scots Church.

Our next fortnight was spent visiting mission stations within reach of Madras such as Arkonam, Chingleput, and Conjeevaram. At the Lady Willingdon Leper Sanatorium we learned that the Indian government had decided to take it over. At Bangalore I visited the United Theological College where Indian pastors taking the B.D. degree are trained. Christianity is stronger numerically and more deeply rooted historically in South India than in any other part of the country and there are many devoted and well trained Indian clergy. We spent several hours at Tambaram.

After crowded weeks around Madras we were almost relieved on 16 October to take the train north to the Central Provinces. At Nagpur we spent some days with the Reverend William Stewart, later Principal of Serampore College and Moderator of the new United Church of North India. From there we went on to Calcutta as guests of the principal, Dr John Kellas, at the Scottish Church College. Though Christian in name and under the Church, most of its students and many members of staff are of other faiths. This seems anomalous. From colleges like this many men go into the professions and industry to take a leading part in society and public affairs. Though they may not become professing Christians they must carry with them certain standards to colour their whole outlook on life.

From the heat, the noise, and the smells of Calcutta it was a relief to go up into the hills at Kalimpong. The last stage was a forty mile drive by car, the first part through flat beautifully wooded country, the second part in the hills by a narrow winding road which ran alongside the magnificent river Teesta, and then finally climbed about 3,000 feet in ten miles, zig-zagging up the mountain side. At the top, we suddenly came out of the woods, and there before us in the distance was the great snow covered Kanchenjunga and the neighbouring peaks. "At Kalimpong we visited the school for Anglo-Indian boys founded by Dr Graham, and I preached in their chapel. We were specially impressed by the small Leper Hospital run by Dr Albert Craig. The reputation of its dedicated doctor had spread far and wide, and lepers travelled long distances on foot from the interior of Tibet, Bhutan, and Nepal, knowing they could count on a welcome and comfort and help. Another wonderful drive took us into Sikkim, for which we had obtained entry passports. There we stayed in the mission house at Gangtok, high in the hillside above the little town, with our only missionary there, Miss Shirras. Unforgettable memories remain. Waking in the early morning and looking out of the window we saw a long leisurely procession of mules and their owners wending their way down the steep descent from Tibet; the women in many-coloured dresses, with long turquoise ear rings, the mules wearing bells whose sound rang out through the still clear mountain air.''

There followed a few delightful days at Darjeeling where we stayed with one of our senior missionaries, the Reverend Harry Duncan, and his wife. On All Saints' Day we got up at 3.30 a.m. Miss Addie joined us and we all drove out to Tiger Hill. We walked the last mile to the summit in darkness and found about thirty people, Lepchas, Nepalis, Tibetans, and three Europeans. After a few minutes the red glow of sunrise began to appear in the east and spread wider and wider, until finally the brilliant orb of the sun rose above the horizon and struck full upon the snow-covered peaks of Kanchenjunga and, slightly further west, Everest. Not a cloud in the sky, and every great peak in the range stood out clear, an unforgettable sight. We stayed till 7 a.m. watching the changing lights and seeing the plains gradually coming into view to the south.

From Darjeeling we travelled into the Eastern Duars to visit one of the most remote and primitive of our mission stations. The people are Animists in belief, simple and friendly, and with minds open to the Christian message. Hundreds had professed the faith under the appealing ministry of the Reverend George McLaren, and there was a spacious compound with a church, a school, and hostels for boys and girls. The bungalow where the McLarens lived was on the edge of the jungle, a simple structure of wood, unpainted and unvarnished, and standing on high stilts. He and I had been at New College together.

The next stage of our meeting took us into a highly sophisticated environment, Allahabad, to a meeting of the United Church of North India. In the evening after our arrival we attended the enthronement of the new Bishop of Lucknow, the Right Reverend Christopher Robinson, in the Anglican Cathedral. Most of the next three days was spent at the General Assembly, where I conveyed greetings from Scotland. Dr. Kellas put forward the report of the Committee on Reunion, commending supplemental ordination as the only way if the Anglicans were to be included. The Assembly recommended integration between church and mission in each area as soon as possible and sent messages of loyalty to the Indian and Pakistan Governments. Scots congregations were invited to join the Church of North India, and to this there was a willing and warm assent. Missionaries came under the jurisdiction of the Church of North India though their salaries were still paid by the Church of Scotland. Twenty years were to pass before the larger cause of Reunion was attained.

After another visit to Nagpur we travelled into the wild country of Bihar. The Santal people, Animists in religion, are simple and largely illiterate. Eye diseases are prevalent and the mission hospital attracts sufferers from far and near. The hospital is incredibly primitive by ordinary western standards and Dr Dempster is as overworked as he is beloved. Round the compound were many open huts or sheds in each of which a family was encamped, since a patient is accompanied by his family who cook his food and look after him. We went into the simple wooden operating theatre. When the doctor was ready an elderly woman was led in by the hand by her husband. He helped her on to the operating table, and when she had lain down, her face and neck were carefully washed. Her husband stood close by. Dr Dempster then operated for cataract. Looking round I noticed that the door was wide open while people watched with intense interest. Then the old lady was helped down from the table and led out by her husband. There was no nurse and only a young man to assist. After watching two operations, I asked Dr Dempster if he did not find it difficult under such conditions and if it was not distracting. "Well," he said, "the conditions are essential in order to give confidence to the people. If I were to operate in secret and behind closed doors, these simple people would be suspicious, and all kinds of rumours might get about, whereas everything I do is open. They can see exactly what happens, and that gives them confidence and trust." As the doctor walked among the groups waiting in hope I felt that here was a continuation of the healing ministry of Jesus as he moved among the sick at the pool of Bethesda.

After driving to Assamol we took the Punjab train to Lucknow. My wife is a great-great-grand-niece of Sir Henry Lawrence and we went to see the Residency and Lawrence's grave. Professor Ahmad Shah, head of the Department of Education at the University, and his wife took us to tea at Government House where we met Mrs Sorajini Naidu. Later we had dinner with Lady Maharaj Singh, whose husband was soon to be the first Indian Governor of Bombay.

After Lucknow it was tempting to get a glimpse of Agra. We engaged a tonga driven by a little old man with a beard, who brandished a whip and lashed it round the flanks of his little old horse. After a two and a half mile drive we came to the great gateway leading to the Taj Mahal. In spite of our having seen it so often in photographs the grandeur of it exceeded all expectations. Its calm dignity and the beauty of the inlaid designs of jade, agate, and yellow and black marble are endlessly fascinating.

Another train journey took us into Rajputana and the old town of Ajmer. It was a place in which both Hindus and Muslims have sacred associations and there had been serious violence. We arrived in the middle of a seventytwo hour curfew. All schools, offices, and shops were shut. On 9 December we heard that the curfew was to be lifted from 10 a.m. to 4 p.m. so that people might buy food. The streets were crowded and soldiers were everywhere with rifles and fixed bayonets. Outside shops police with batons kept order. Next day, following the funeral of a Hindu policeman who had been murdered, a Muslim was killed and his shop looted and burned. A twentyfour hour curfew was imposed but we could see smoke rising in columns from parts of the old city. Tension in the mission compound was heightened by the arrival of the bearer's whole family in a tonga. Mrs Drummond gave them a house in the servants' quarters but, as they were Muslims, the other Indians felt it created a danger. They stood about in a group talking till dusk. The Reverend Dr Jack Drummond, with whom we stayed, was an old friend of mine. Despite the disturbances he took us round the church, hospital, and mission schools and some of the splendid buildings of the city.

In the Punjab, where next I had to go, massacres and fighting had been specially bad. No trains were running to the north and it was not easy even to get a seat on a plane. Jack and Helen Drummond pressed my wife to stay with them in my absence and took her to Jodhpur for part of the time. After a brief visit to our missionaries in Jaipur, I took a plane to New Delhi. Delhi was very unsettled and there were rumours of a possible attempted coup by the Sikhs. The streets seemed full of magnificent bearded men in turbans.

If there was one person in India whom I would like to meet it was Mahatma Gandhi. Now that I found myself in Delhi the idea came to me. My old cousin, Emily Kinnaird, who had died only a few months previously, was a life long friend of India and of Gandhi. I made contact with his secretary and introduced myself. To my great delight he told me that Gandhi had been travelling a good deal lately, visiting refugee camps for both Hindus and Muslims, but that he was returning home that afternoon. At 5 p.m. I presented myself at Birla House. There was a spacious garden and rather to my surprise the gates were wide open and many were going in and out. He had refused any security precautions and wished to be accessible to all.

As soon as I gave my name I was escorted along a passage and into a quiet dimly lit room. It was only after a moment that I saw the Mahatma sitting near the wall on the floor, a small man, wizened and wrinkled and incredibly thin, dressed in a plain white cotton garment, and with his spinning wheel beside him. "Shall I have a chair brought for you, Mr Davidson?" he said. But I asked if I might sit beside him on the floor. There was an atmosphere of stillness and peace in the room. He began at once to talk with affection of Emily Kinnaird and asked me about her last illness, as he had not heard of her death. He wanted to know why I was in India and to hear of the mission stations. I asked him, "Is the future of Indian Christianity and mission work secure for the future?" He said, "I can't answer that question. But what I would say is, if it is God's will that the Christian missionaries remain in India, then they will go on against however terrible odds. If it is God's will that the missionaries should not remain, then they will have to go. But history doesn't suggest that it will work out in that way."

As our conversation finished he said that they always had prayers in the garden at that hour and invited me to accompany him. In the garden about two hundred and fifty people of all ranks and conditions were waiting on the lawn. Prayers were chanted first in Urdu, then in Hindi. The Mahatma, seated on a divan in a little red brick pavilion, then spoke to the assembly for fifteen minutes on the evacuation of Muslims and Hindus (of which he strongly disapproved) and about food and cloth controls and about the black market. He was a very impressive person in his combination of utter simplicity of life, shrewdness of practical judgement, and spirituality of outlook. His was the one voice to which the whole of divided India listened, giving very wise counsel, utterly above communal differences.

As soon as he had finished speaking he walked back to the house with his arms on the shoulders of two grand-daughters. Little did I think that only a month later he would be attacked and killed at the same hour in that garden. I felt that I had had the privilege of seeing face to face a man of God and one of the eight or ten supreme figures of the world of our time.

Next morning I had to fly to Lahore and from there to our mission stations at Gujerat, Jalalpur, and Daska. Everywhere the Hindus had been massacred and their shops and houses burned to the ground. At our hospital in Jalalpur in insecurity and bitterness, Dr Skinner and his wife and very small staff courageously carried on with victims of violence being constantly brought in to increase the pressure in the wards. We drove out to a refugee camp two miles from the town and were conducted round it. There were ten thousand refugees there, all evacuated from the East Punjab and other parts of India. All were in some sort of shelter, some in large school buildings, the rest in rough huts made of reeds and grass. There was a hospital, though rough and primitive, and over eighty smallpox cases were isolated. Government provision of food, clothes, blankets, and medical supplies were sufficient to give moderate comfort. As soon as possible refugee families were drafted out to villages where departing Hindus had left land and houses. Many missionaries felt isolated and saddened by the tragic happenings which were tearing the community to pieces. At Lahore I had a long talk with the bishop, Dr Barnes. He was very optimistic about the future of Christian schools and hospitals but felt that no one could say what would be the attitude of the Pakistan government to evangelism.

After spending Christmas in the hospitable home of the Reverend Leslie Scott, Principal of Murray College, Sialkot, and meeting the missionaries there I returned for a day to New Delhi. I drove out to the Secretariat and walked about, looking at the enormous buildings, impressive by their very size. All was quiet and dignified in the National Legislative Assembly Hall. A portrait of Mahatma Gandhi hung above the President's chair. In the Anglican Cathedral of the Redemption I said prayers for India and Pakistan. Next day I returned to Rajputana where my wife had been looked after by the Drummonds. Pandit Nehru came to Ajmer to see the civic authorities and address the people after the disturbances. He addressed a mass meeting of about twenty thousand in the polo ground. We listened and watched from the roof of the Boys' High School, which was just behind the platform. He spoke for half an hour and got complete attention, but not much acclamation, perhaps because he said that Ajmer had stained its good name in recent weeks. I admired his courage, both in speaking with such directness, and because afterwards he walked through the mixed crowd to his car with almost no police protection and ignoring the risk of attack in a situation full of tension.

Before leaving Rajputana we went to spend a few days with one of our most senior missionaries, the Reverend James Runciman, and his wife in Udaipur, one of the most beautiful places in India. In the afternoon we were rowed very slowly down the lake, past the old walled city whose houses and temples and huge palaces with their domes and towers were shimmering white in the sunlight. On the further shore turtles and a young crocodile were basking in the sun; painted storks, cranes, and herons stood in the shallow water, and flights of parakeets, teal, and cormorants passed overhead. We put ashore on an island where a little old summer palace stands, and had tea among the pillars of a small white marble pavilion on the edge of the lake. Beside it was a garden of roses, cinerarias, and bougainvillia, and beyond that a little orchard of bananas, paprika, and orange trees. The whole scene was magical, and one seemed to have stepped altogether out of time. This was enhanced by the fact that the Maharani, a friend of Mr Runciman, had put a two-horse carriage at his disposal during our visit, so that we drove about in old fashioned state, with a postillion standing behind and an elderly bearded coachman in uniform on the box.

Our journeying was drawing to an end. After visits to Jalna and Poona, we found ourselves back at Wilson College, Bombay for a last week of speaking, preaching, and consultation. I felt thankful that I had been able to fulfil my commission, visiting all eight separate areas of our Scottish missions and almost every post. The diversity was remarkable. Some missionaries lived in large sophisticated cities; others in remote places among simple people and in primitive conditions. Some met a ready response; others faced prejudice or apathy. But everywhere the seed was being faithfully sown. Best of all, everywhere one could see an Indian Christian Church which would gradually be able to stand on its own feet. The greatest need was for a larger number of well-trained Indian and Pakistani pastors who could take responsibility and give leadership. Already this was beginning to happen and was raising new questions about the role of the missionary. Independence underlined the issue.

Older missionaries were sometime accused of paternalism. In earlier days this was natural and not undesirable, but already in 1948 it could be seen that the missionary must be less a leader and more a friend. This change called for patience, humility, and unselfishness. In several places we could see this partnership already in practice. In every post we visited these questions were eagerly discussed. It was possible to make a fuller report when we returned home than could be conveyed by letters. The kindness my wife and I received in every mission station sent us home with a sense of new friendship in many a distant bungalow and hospital and school.

On Saturday, 30 January, our last day in Bombay, Gandhi came as usual into the grounds of Birla House to attend prayers. He was leaning on the shoulder of his grand-niece, Maru. As he was going up the steps to the prayer platform a Hindu youth, a Brahmin from Poona, suddenly broke through the assembled congregation and fired three shots at the Mahatma. Within a few minutes he died. The news swept through the country, causing almost incredulous horror and grief. Bombay was like a city of the dead; all shops and offices closed, no cars or taxis were on the streets, and a strange silence everywhere. At 8.30 Pandit Nehru spoke to the nation on the radio, at 10 at the special request of the students at Wilson College we went to the large men's hostel for a short service. Dr Kellock, Professor Taylor, the Warden, two of the students, and I all spoke briefly. As we sang Gandhi's favourite hymn, "When I survey the wondrous cross", tears were streaming down the cheeks of many students. They had also lost their irreplaceable leader and hero, father and friend. Our ship, once again the *Celicia*, sailed next day. I obtained permission from the Captain to hold a short memorial service. The Government announced a period of thirteen days of mourning throughout India.

It was a pleasant voyage home. There were no fewer than seven Indian Ecclesiastical Chaplains returning home as a result of independence. General Sir Rob Lockhart had spent almost all his soldiering life in India, latterly as Commander-in-Chief, and was leaving with many regrets. He spoke very interestingly about both Nehru and Patel. He also said that, contrary to rumours, the Indian troops led by British officers, had behaved extraordinarily well during the communal riots.

The diary records another pleasant incident. "Buchanan, the deck steward, told me that the chief baker on the ship was a member of our Cathedral congregation, so I went down to the bake-house and found it was Orr, of Morrin Square. He was very pleased to see me, and I told him how everyone on board enjoyed his morning rolls made of good white flour, after the sour Indian bread. He showed us all the different gadgets in the bakery and then took us to his cabin and gave us tea and showed photographs of his family."

Returning to Glasgow in the spring of 1948 I was plunged at once into the crowded ongoing life of the city. Everything at the Cathedral had gone well under the care of Principal Fulton and the two assistant ministers, George MacLean Henderson and Pat Moffett. The presbytery had generously allowed me two months' longer absence than had been expected. Interest in India and Pakistan in those months after independence was keen. I was called upon to speak not only to the Foreign Mission Committee, the General Assembly, and the presbytery, but also on the radio and at gatherings of all sorts. It had been an unforgettable experience and one which made a profound impression on all my thinking about the powerful appeal of the Christian Gospel and the significance of the other great faiths of the world. In every continent, in countless ways, men and women reach out towards God.

8

Committees and Projects

Apart from church life in Glasgow I spent much time on committees of our General Assembly. As meetings were in Edinburgh this meant a good deal of travelling, but fortunately I have always been able to write in the train, so that time was not wasted. There was a tension always between the claims of one's own city and the demands of committee work. Yet a part can be taken in the wider work of the Church only through committees with men and women from different parts and of different points of view.

For six years the convenership of the Church and Nation Committee took much of my time. Its remit was a large one: "The Committee on Church and Nation shall watch over those developments in the nation's life in which moral and spiritual considerations specially arise, and shall consider what action the Church from time to time might be advised to take to further the highest interest of the people." It symbolised the concern of the Church in the whole life of the country. There have been criticisms about this remit and suggestions that it may lead the Church into purely secular areas. Yet human life is a unity and the Christian who is a member of the Church is also a citizen of the world. Sacred and secular are inextricably interwoven. Year by year the Committee presents its conclusions on a varied range of problems; depopulation of the Highlands, Scottish devolution, unemployment, old age pensions, nuclear warfare and the concept of a 'just war', the international arms race, road safety, standards in broadcasting, social problems created by North Sea oil, the mentally handicapped, conditions in farming, aid to developing Africa, the Christian use of Sunday, and better human relations in industry.

There are always on the Committee elders of knowledge and experience in public service and we rely on their specialised views. The Committee's reports are published some weeks before the General Assembly and are often very fully published in the press. Usually the debate occupies a day and frequently a representative of some government department can be seen listening in the gallery. Copies of the report are sent to the Prime Minister, senior ministers in certain departments, and all Scottish Members of Parliament. It encourages all members of the Church to direct their thinking on the nation's welfare.

Another sphere of interest was the Inter-Church Relations Committee of which I was a member for many years and Convener for five. I am convinced that the ecumenical movement is the outstanding feature of religious life in our century. Its aims and hopes are so large that anyone involved must think in long scale terms, must be ready for achievements and disappointments, and conscious that these hopes can never be fulfilled by human efforts alone but only by the guidance of the Holy Spirit.

My first interest goes back to the meeting in Edinburgh in 1937 of the Second World Conference on Faith and Order under Dr Arthur C. Headlam, the Bishop of Gloucester. It was a new experience to find oneself in free discussion with representatives of the Orthodox Churches, the Lutherans, the Anglicans, and the Free Churches. Ecumenical discussion was more cautious at that time, personal relations were less familiar, and often differences were partly concealed under excessive courtesy of manner and speech. Representatives of the Orthodox Church were extremely reserved, almost always sat together in a group and, when their views had to be expressed, only one spoke for all. Clearly they had not made up their minds about the safety of such gatherings, and seemed less ready to listen than to state the unchangeable position of their own tradition. How strangely different from today, when Orthodox influence is one of the strongest in the World Council of Churches.

My interest had been greatly increased by my presence at the reunion of the Churches in South India in 1947. Five months of contact with church leaders in all parts of India made me more conscious than ever of the tragedy of the divisions in the Christian family. Our divisions in Western Europe have deep historical roots, but we have carried these rivalries into lands where they have no roots and cannot properly be understood. Reunion in South India and later in North India has given eloquent response and pointed "a more excellent way" to the older Churches of the West. At the Faith and Order Conference at the University of Lund in Sweden in August 1952, I sat in a conclave of church leaders and scholars from many lands and traditions. A distinguished bishop of the Swedish Church was chairman and Professor Leonard Hodgson of Oxford, secretary. In our group from the Church of Scotland were Professor Donald Baillie, Dr A.C. Craig, Sir Randal Philip, and myself.

After an opening assembly at the University on 16 August and worship in the evening there was a celebration of the eucharist. My diary records, "To the cathedral at 10 a.m. for High Mass, at which all delegates to the Conference had been invited to receive communion. A vast congregation, filling every pew, and many people even sitting on the long flight of steps up to the altar. The Dean of Lund celebrated and the Bishop, Dr Nygren, preached a most impressive sermon on the cleansing of the temple.''

For working days the Conference was divided into sections. To my satisfaction I was allocated to the section concerned with "ways of worship," with Bishop Hans Lillie of Germany as chairman, and the Reverend Marcus Ward and the Reverend C. Chandra of India as secretaries. Dr Leslie Cook of the English Congregational Church and I were asked to write those parts of the report dealing with "Fundamental Points of Agreement" and "The Communion of Saints.'' One glimpsed the wideness and wealth of the Church Catholic as compared with the heritage of any single part. At full sessions we heard memorable addresses from Professor Josef Hromadka of Czechoslovakia, Dr D.T. Niles of Sri Lanka, Bishop John Peter of Hungary, Pastor M. Maury of France, and Dr Douglas Horton of England. The closing act was a splendid service of thanksgiving in the Cathedral on the evening of 28 August. Of all its pronouncements the most lasting was the "Lund Dictum", calling on the different Churches to act together on every occasion except when strongly held principles forbad it.

The Lund Conference encouraged more frequent visits between Churches of different countries. I have been a delegate of our Church to Norway, Sweden, Denmark, and Finland. At Uppsala our host was Archbishop Hultgren. In a country house on an island in Denmark against a background of sea and sky and living as a group of friends, one discovered how slim are the ecclesiastical barriers between us and how strong the central Christian beliefs that bind us together. One result is that the Church of Sweden and the Church of Scotland are now in full communion. A similar recognition has been achieved between some of the Lutheran (and all of the United) Churches in Germany and every Reformed Church on the continent. In our own country ecumenical progress has been slow. In spite of the leadership of almost all of its bishops, the Church of England has failed to achieve union with the Methodist Church and in Scotland the General Assembly by a small majority refused union with the Congregationalists. Yet discussion continues and friendship grows, and there are encouraging signs.

I was also for a good many years a member, and for a time one of the Vice-Presidents, of the British Council of Churches. I doubt if it exerts much influence and the studies it produces are seldom widely known, but it is a significant institution in the contemporary Christian scene. Representative of almost all the Churches except the Roman Catholic, it provides a meeting place where most of the principal problems of our time are discussed. Sometimes a common mind is easily reached. At other times the debates are highly controversial. But the clash of opinions is stimulating and behind the differences is a genuine respect for views other than one's own, a readiness to listen, and occasionally the discovery that one's own opinion must be changed. The few Quaker members speak seldom, but always with effect, looking at every question in depth.

I sat in the Council under two Presidents, Archbishop Fisher and Archbishop Ramsey. They presented a total contrast in temperament and chairmanship. Geoffrey Fisher was a man of out-going friendliness who created an atmosphere of freedom in discussion, but he had been a headmaster, and ever and again the authoritarian attitude re-asserted itself. He would intervene in such a tone as to suggest that no other view was worth hearing. Usually only one other Anglican dared to argue: Mrs Fisher, a very charming and able woman, did not hesitate to cross swords with the Archbishop, often with softening effect. Michael Ramsey had equal distinction but different gifts. He did not hesitate to shew when business bored him. He deliberately withdrew his interest and passed into a coma for a time; but as soon as vital discussion began again he was instantly alert. It was almost as though he had his sub-conscious mind as well trained as his conscious.

Perhaps the chief value of the British Council of Churches is as an instrument enabling the Churches in our country to speak with one voice on matters of supreme import in the life of the nation. There is reason to believe that this voice is increasingly listened to in many quarters, and with respect, because it represents united Christian thinking unspoilt by sectarian prejudices. It has always surprised me that the Council receives such meagre notice in the press. Is it because the Churches no longer hold the place they did? Or is it because many editors wrongly assume that religious views have no interest for their readers?

For some ten years I was chairman of the Scottish Churches Ecumenical Committee. It was felt that we should secure a site for a Retreat House and Ecumenical Centre, one convenient for access and possessing Christian associations. In 1955 we discovered it. Dunblane was within easy reach of our cities, and had been the seat of a mediaeval bishopric. Its ancient Cathedral above the Allan Water holds an atmosphere of serenity and is a focus of activity. Close by is a row of small eighteenth century houses. They were dilapidated and condemned for demolition, but simple and charming, and characteristic of their period. Some years before they had been purchased by The Friends of Dunblane Cathedral but there had been no funds to put them in order. Satisfactory decisions were reached. The Friends presented the houses to our Ecumenical Committee, the town council agreed to withdraw the demolition order if funds could be found to restore them, and a generous donor, Major David Russell, offered £10,000. The Historic Buildings Council made a grant. An appeal fund was set up under Lord Balerno, and plans for reconstruction were prepared by Mr Eric Stevenson.

So, after many delays the Scottish Churches House was brought into being in 1961, an institution unique in character, being jointly owned by all the Churches in Scotland except the Roman Catholic. Its purpose has been well described by a former Warden, the Rev. J. Wilson McLeod, "It is a visible sign of unity, a symbol for all to see of a greater unity that will be. Set in the very centre of Scotland, it looks out on the total life of Scotland.... and further afield — at the life of the whole world.... It is a centre of study and discussion, where groups can come to a better understanding of the problems of the world today, and especially where Christians can come to a realization of their responsible Christian contribution.... It exists to be a place of meeting and reconciliation." We were fortunate in securing as the first Warden the Reverend Ian Fraser. It has proved itself a meeting ground in which those of many Christian traditions are helped to forget old separations and find how much they have in common. As I write this a new appeal for funds is being launched to enlarge and improve the house. My diary of 19 November 1956 records: "A momentous decision and act of faith. Pray God it may be justified." I think it has been.

It was decided to initiate a Multi-Lateral Church Conversation in Scotland among all those willing to take part. This Conversation, of which I was asked to be chairman, consisted of members of the Episcopal Church in Scotland, the Methodist Church, the Congregational Union, the United Free Church, the Churches of Christ, and the Church of Scotland, our remit being to prepare a basis and plan of union for Churches in Scotland. Interim reports have been published on "The Faith of the Church", "Ministry", and "Worship and Sacraments", and received by the constituent Churches with varying degrees of approval and criticism. More growing together is needed, and especially prayer. A similar commission has now been set up in England.

No less encouraging has been an increasing degree of friendship between the Church of Scotland and the Roman Catholic community. On both sides there had been suspicion and often open hostility, but in recent times and, more especially, since the time of the gentle and saintly Pope John, the whole ecumenical climate has changed. Ministers of the different communions develop personal friendships. Practical action is taken together in many spheres, and theological discussion is being promoted instead of avoided. This was symbolised by a recent happening which could probably not have taken place even five years ago. After a private exchange of views the Inter-Church Relations Committee of the Assembly for the first time asked for permission to invite an observer of the Roman Catholic Church to address the General Assembly. By a large majority it was accepted and the Roman Catholic authorities warmly agreed. In May 1975 for the first time for four hundred years the General Assembly welcomed a dignitary "from the other side" in the person of the Most Reverend James Winning, Roman Catholic Archbishop of Glasgow. His notable address, frank, friendly, and profoundly Christian in tone, moved the Assembly to a response beyond all expectations. The future is in God's hands. As Cardinal Suenens of Belgium has put it, "We must be free enough to understand today what the Spirit is saying to the Churches. The Church is not faithful to itself unless it is ready at every moment for the surprises of the Holy Spirit and the unexpectedness of God."

In 1950 I accepted an invitation from the British Broadcasting Council to become chairman of their Religious Advisory Committee for Scotland in succession to the Very Reverend Professor John Baillie. This was a time of unusual interest, involving experiments and new lines of policy. One of the most important was the question of whether broadcasting and televising of holy communion should be permitted. Opinions differed. There were strong arguments on each side. It could be held that the sacrament is a mystery given by Christ to His people, to be understood and partaken only by those actually present. To listen to a broadcast could be no substitute. On the other hand it was argued that the broadcasting of a sacramental occasion would bring comfort to many who could not attend, and that even the hearing of the time honoured words might speak to those who sat lightly to spiritual things. Now, some twenty years later, when we have become accustomed to television of the sacraments, the arguments seem strange and outmoded. Yet I am not sure that something is not lost in permitting them to be viewed simply from the attitude of a spectator. But this is not the common opinion.

Discussion was long and careful. In the end it was felt that the only course was to allow such a service and judge by the reactions. A country church was the first selected, Dunbarney Parish Church, on 5 February 1954 with Dr T.B. Stewart Thomson as the celebrant. Out of over a hundred letters received by the B.B.C. only two were critical. It was appreciated by the elderly and the invalids and many ministers and elders were impressed.

After a conference between the B.B.C. and the Church of Scotland Committee on Public Worship and Aids to Devotion my diary records: "We almost all regret its coming, but agree that it is unavoidable." Not long afterwards we had a televised service in our own Cathedral on Easter Day. I found the brilliant lighting and cameras distracting at first, but the Easter hymns and organ music were lovely and the large congregation reverent. With the full liturgy and sermon the service lasted for an hour and fifteen minutes. Since then services of baptism, confirmation, and holy communion have frequently been shewn on television and accepted in most denominations. They are no substitute for attendance in a worshipping congregation, the proper setting for the Gospel sacraments.

Another committee which involved much time and thought and of which I acted as chairman was a Commission set up by the General Assembly in 1954 to "investigate the matter of Spiritual Healing, to examine the theological implications, and formulate, with the approval of the General Assembly, definite guidance for both ministers and laymen of the Church." The Commission consisted of six medical men, two advocates, one deaconess, Mrs McGillivray, and eleven parish ministers and theological professors. Among the medical men were doctors and surgeons such as Sir David Henderson, Professor Stanley Alstead, and Mr G.H. Stevenson. Among the lawyers were Mr Harald R. Leslie, Q.C., now Lord Birsay, and among the clergy Professor Donald Baillie, Professor J.S. Stewart, Dr A.C. Craig, Reverend J.C. Peddie, Professor W.R. Forrester, Professor David Cairns, and the Reverend J.A.C. Murray. The secretary was the Reverend Dr T. Crouther Gordon.

One more indication of the uncertainty felt by many today as to the role of the ordained minister was the claim of some doctors that probably more people with intimate problems turned to them for advice. We had some twenty meetings altogether and also held conferences with those concerned in spiritual healing. In the concluding paragraph of the final report we said, "The revival of interest in healing effected by faith and prayer is to be welcomed. It is possibly a part of the Church's ministry which has been allowed to fall into the background alike in thought and practice, and this new interest in the subject is serving also to recall us to a recognition of the vital importance of the pastoral function of the ministry. A modern city minister is often tempted by the innumerable demands upon his time, by the supervision of congregational organisations, the work of Church committees, and manifold other requests for his services, to let pastoral visitation take second place or third place, or even be almost altogether crowded out.

"Those engaged in the ministry of spiritual healing are reminding us afresh of the value of the individual and the need for personal concern and compassion. At the same time we feel it is only right to point out once again that bodily and mental healing, which is normally the task of the physician and surgeon, should never be regarded as the primary concern of the minister of religion. It is certainly his duty at all times to intercede for those who are ill, and this duty is recognised in every branch of the Church. But in the thought and work of the minister, spiritual healing will always take precedence over physical healing as the main concern of the pastoral office. To Christ our Lord Himself, as has been seen, the supreme tragedy is sin, the evil tendency, the evil desire, the evil habit, which separates men and women from God. The primary objective, therefore, in all pastoral work must be the curing of men of the great universal fact of sin, and the bringing them to that reconciliation and daily fellowship with God which will enable them to face all the experience of life and the ultimate experience of death with complete faith and serenity.''

The Committee welcomed co-operation between ministers and doctors and emphasised the duty of intercession for the sick. It discouraged special services of healing. It thanked God for those who were conscious of a special call to minister to the sick by laying on of hands or the use of unction, but urged them to use discretion and always to consult with the patient's doctor. Stress should not be laid exclusively on mere physical cure. Before spiritual healing took place the patient should be instructed that the only way of receiving such treatment is a cheerful acceptance of God's will, whatever that may be.

In the late forties the need for devolution of power and responsibility to Scotland in the conduct of its own affairs sprang into prominence. Scottish affairs received too little consideration in London and decisions were made by men with little knowledge of Scotland, its needs and traditions. While some believed the only answer was separation others, strongly opposed to separation, yet believed that a large measure of devolution was urgently necessary. A leader was found in John M. McCormick, a lawyer, an able speaker, a clear thinker, and a man of passionate conviction. Under his inspiration a Scottish National Assembly met in Edinburgh on Saturday 29 October 1949 to launch a Covenant demanding a Scottish Parliament to deal with Scottish domestic affairs within the framework of the United Kingdom and in loyalty to the Crown. About six hundred delegates assembled, from all parts and every party. The Lord Provost of Edinburgh welcomed us. The speakers were the Duke of Montrose, John Cameron, now Lord Cameron, James Bridie the playwright, Mrs Pryde, D. Gray, the chairman of the Scottish Liberal Party, and myself. The meeting was enthusiastic. There were full reports in the press and leaders in both *The Scotsman* and *The Glasgow Herald,* the former favourable, the latter critical.

The subsequent response was astonishing. I quote from my diary. ''14 January 1950: To a meeting of the Scottish Covenant Committee. The meeting lasted for more than two and a half hours, and we discussed future policy at great length. John McCormick in the chair, and as usual very quiet and businesslike. About 70,000 have now signed the Scottish Covenant, and there is very wide and continuing interest.'' ''Saturday 22 April 1950: To Edinburgh to attend the Fourth National Assembly. I said an opening prayer — for the first time, by the special wish of the Executive Committee. J. McCormick was in the chair, and about 1,000 delegates present. First, speeches by the Duke of Montrose, Mr Ross McLean, K.C., William Power, the journalist, Sir George Ogilvie Forbes, and then general discussion. In the afternoon, Professor Dewar Gibb spoke, and also the Master of Belhaven, the Earl of Mansfield, MacLean of Lochbuie, and many others of all political parties. Finally we passed a resolution (only two dissenting) to approach the Prime Minister and leaders of other parties with a view to negotiation for a Scottish Parliament to deal with Scottish affairs."

"Monday 29 May: To the General Assembly directly after breakfast. The report of the Church and Nation Committee took the whole morning. An addendum on the necessity for a Royal Commission on Scottish Affairs, proposed by Professor James Pitt-Watson and seconded by myself, caused some controversy but in the end was accepted by a large majority." John McCormick had been elected Rector of Glasgow University and was becoming well known. He chaired a meeting of the Covenant Committee on 23 January 1951 which lasted three hours. A cleavage of opinion appeared but McCormick was prepared for compromise and in the end moderation prevailed. A meeting in March decided to persuade as many as possible of the two million signatories to join a Covenant Association to work for Scottish self government on domestic questions.

At one such meeting I said, "The great issue which has brought us here today is not a matter of party politics. Nor is it a matter of narrow nationalism. It would be a folly to disown our debt or our loyalty to the larger inheritance of Great Britain which has brought, and still brings us, numberless advantages and immense enrichment. The one grand assumption behind this whole meeting is that Scotland is not a province but a nation — a nation with a distinctive ethos, heritage, traditions, customs of its own. It shows itself not only in our educational system, our legal system, our mode of Church government, but in countless small customs and habits of everyday life. It used to show itself, though perhaps less today, in certain qualities of character and outlook — thrift, industry, independence, personal pride. The great steam roller of centralisation is slowly ironing out, or should one say, crushing out, all local individuality, idiosyncrasy, responsibility, initiative. A completely London-centred and London-controlled administrative machine has little time to recognise or adapt itself to the Scottish soil and landscape. The Covenant being launched today at this National Assembly is at least an attempt to arrest the fatal advance of that steam roller. I believe that if we in Scotland had greater control in our own domestic affairs it would stimulate, as nothing else could do, not only industrial initiative but cultural zest and moral vigour. More important than economic revival is spiritual revival. Although accidental it is yet significant that we should be meeting today within the walls of the Assembly Hall of the Church of Scotland. For the Church is perhaps the greatest remaining repository of our Scottish national sentiment and self-consciousness, and the true symbol of the national character and temperament. Strong and profound religious convictions have been the basic elements in Scottish life and character through all its most vital periods. And only a re-discovery of our Christian heritage, values, and convictions will provide the necessary inspiration and dynamic for a revival of the Scottish nation in the widest sense of the word.''

At the moment when the movement seemed to be making real progress an unfortunate event occurred. Two young men stole the Stone of Destiny from under the Coronation Chair in Westminster Abbey. A few secretly admired the audacious act, but the great majority were horrified. It was some weeks before the stone was recovered. It had been placed in the ruins of Arbroath Abbey. McCormick's death soon after was an even more grievous blow. Today, after a kind of uneasy interlude, the demand has been more vigorously revived and seems likely to result in some real structure of value and significance.

9

Leisure and Life in Glasgow

Everyone needs release at times, not only from work, but from city life. When we could my wife and I would escape to the Campsie Fells, Loch Lomond, or the Clyde coast, and once when walking near Houston we noticed an old stone tower being used as a store for machinery and tools. It could easily have been converted into a small house so, taking courage, we knocked at the farm house door and asked if the farmer would sell and at what price. He had not thought of selling but promptly named an exorbitant price and this ended the conversation. Yet the idea had been placed in our minds. In the late middle ages many small towers had been built by lairds, so we asked a friend, Ian Lindsay, the architect, to suggest a small tower in reasonable condition and not too far from Glasgow. He named Hallbar in Lanarkshire, some twenty miles from Glasgow in orchard country, and arranged that we should meet the estate factor there.

When we reached the spot we discovered the tower completely surrounded by trees and shrubs, with long grass and brambles growing to the door step. It had not been inhabited for sixty years. Most of the glass in the windows had gone; several doors were missing; the floor of an upper room had fallen in; and the stone roof was in a sad state. But the old house itself, dating from the sixteenth century, had great character and was a very ingenious piece of architecture. Sixty feet in height, it was perfectly square, each side measuring twenty four feet. The walls were five feet thick and contained sections of the stairs. At ground level the entrance led into a vaulted store which may have sheltered cattle in time of danger. On the first floor was the main room, the hall, with a huge open fireplace and a large chimney. After this were two other rooms, each fourteen feet square. The final staircase opened on to small battlements and another very pleasant room with an ornamental window from which could be had wide views across the rolling landscape. Weeds and even small trees were growing on the battlements and between the slabs of the roof.

As we stood in conversation the factor said, "I don't suppose it is of any use to you." We exchanged glances and I said, "It is exactly what we have been looking for." The owner, Major Simon Lockhart-Macdonald, had only recently succeeded to a large estate and had not yet seen

Hallbar, but as it had been in the possession of his family for more than 300 years he was disinclined to sell. Very generously he agreed to lease it indefinitely to us for the nominal sum of £1 per annum, on the understanding that he should be involved in no expense. This was ideal. The restoration of the fascinating old building and the improvement of its surroundings was to be a leisure ploy for the next few years. The tower was completely secluded, even from the nearest cottage. It stood on a triangular peninsula of land sloping steeply to two small streams which joined further down the hill. There were a few fine trees, but far too much undergrowth calling for clearing. Behind the old house was an orchard of plum and apple trees belonging to a nearby farmer. By day the only sounds were the voices of birds and the sound of the Fidler Burn, and by night the owls among the trees.

There were a hundred things to do but first we had to make it possible to sleep there occasionally. Just after the war it was difficult to get building materials, but by the good offices of Ian Lindsay large slabs of Caithness slate were sent from the north and chimed in well with the original stone roof. The erection of half a dozen enormous beams on to the stone corbels to support a new floor for the middle room was a delicate operation. The battlements had to be cleared and dust and debris removed from the stairs, the two garde-robes, and the fireplace.

Almost nothing could be carried up the narrow steep stairs so it was a problem to install furniture. Long ropes were lowered from the battlements, and large pieces of furniture such as beds and armchairs were hoisted up and in at the windows. A firm of joiners in Lanark installed glass in the windows and in early spring we decided to spend our first night at the tower. We arrived on a wet and stormy afternoon to discover that no glass was yet in our bedroom window on the third floor. When we climbed the stair to bed it was difficult to keep the flickering oil lamp alight, the cold was intense, and the wind among the trees made them creak and groan. In spite of all, we managed to sleep. In the dim light of morning my wife whispered, ''I hear the sound of wings.'' When morning came we found that a pigeon had laid an egg on the corner of the window sill. For sixty years pigeons has been the only residents. Who could blame them for attempting to hold on to their long tenancy?

Generations of jackdaws had used the top section of the chimney for building their nests, but when it had been cleaned — with considerable difficulty — by a chimney sweep from Carluke the fire in the wide old grate burned magnificently. We had an ample supply of wood from our small domain; sawing logs was a pleasant change of work and on arrival our first task was always to light a good fire. In the beginning the only water came from a nearby stream and had to be boiled, but after a few months we had a pipe connected to the main supply some three hundred yards away. This gave us cold water in the house and a touch of modern civilization.

We contrived to secure a day and often a night at the tower in most weeks. Apart from the restoration of the quaint old house itself the improvement of our little piece of land called for hard manual labour. The grass which covered what had been the old courtyard had to be scythed. Many small trees had to be cut down and masses of undergrowth and brambles cleared to give light and air. All was made doubly arduous as the hillside from the plateau down to the streams was on a slope of about 45°. One went stumbling and slipping. Gradually the place began to look cared for. One day Bill Buchan, the son of Lord Tweedsmuir, whose little son Toby I had recently christened, appeared with a few hundred daffodil bulbs as a present. Every April afterwards they made our hill top festive. Other friends came and we would have lunch on a rough wooden table in the open air or tea in front of a log fire in the hall upstairs.

New friends were made in the surrounding countryside, the Craigs of Milnwood, the Patersons of Chapel Farm, or the Stewarts of Brierneuk. We came to know Sir John and Lady Colville, later to become Lord and Lady Clydesmuir, of Braidwood House only two miles away. A former Governor of Bombay and at one time Secretary of State for Scotland, he was a man of varied gifts and interests and found great pleasure in playing the organ in their library. Through three generations their family have been among our most intimate and valued friends. Another new friend was the late Reverend Cornelius Smith, parish minister of Crossford, a man of scholarship and quiet charm. From his manse windows he could see smoke rising from our chimney to tell him that we were "in residence." He was a keen beekeeper and his honey was the darkest in colour and richest in taste I have ever eaten.

Our longer holidays were almost always spent at our own house in Strathspey. By long custom we invited a succession of distinguished churchmen to preach in the Cathedral in summer while pastoral work was carried on by the two assistant ministers. This enabled me to take part of July and August in the North, and we usually had ten days directly after Easter. Friends came to see us and the house was full. John Baillie, Professor of Divinity at Edinburgh and his brother Donald, Professor of Systematic Theology at St Andrews, stayed with us. Another guest was Dr John MacNab, Moderator of the Presbyterian Church of Canada. The two Baillie brothers, one happily married, the other a bachelor, were unusually devoted, and it was charming to see them together, affectionately teasing each other, and whenever possible finding an excuse for an argument. Both were distinguished theologians, greatly honoured and loved by students. Curiously enough it was Donald, the bachelor, who was more human and approachable, probably because he had been a parish minister before going to a chair, whereas John had been an academic all his life. Other friends and relatives came until we returned refreshed from the heather, the birch trees, and the river.

So the years went by filled with parish work and special services, before a General Election, to celebrate the silver jubilee of broadcasting, a crowded service for the theatres and cinemas of the city, a memorial service for Harry Lauder, and many others.

In the spring of 1955 Dr Billy Graham came to Glasgow. Reports of his campaigns in London and elsewhere had evoked different reactions. Some were critical of what they regarded as emotionalism and a fundamentalist view of the Bible. Others were enthusiastic. Wherever he held his meetings, they were attended by thousands. Though I did not fully share his approach I was bound to welcome any movement that would bring any of the careless into touch with God and combat the spiritual apathy of our time.

A service of dedication was held in the Cathedral for all taking part in the All-Scotland Crusade. The Reverend Tom Allan, a young minister of unusual ability and spiritual fervour, who had been the Crusade's chief organiser, led the prayers, a Member of Parliament, John Henderson, read the lessons, while I preached and welcomed Dr Graham, who "spoke for about five minutes, straightforward, simple, sincere, and obviously a man of passionate Christian conviction." This first impression was confirmed in the weeks that followed, and remains unchanged.

On the opening night at the Kelvin Hall the huge arena was crowded with an audience of eighteen thousand. There was brilliant lighting and an elaborate broadcasting apparatus. A choir of twelve hundred sang mission hymns and the twentythird psalm. Dr Billy Graham preached for about forty minutes on Faith, finishing with a personal appeal for decision for Christ. While the choir softly sang, "Just as I am without one plea, but that Thy blood was shed for me", three hundred and forty men and women came forward, and were then directed to a side hall for personal talks with counsellors. There was no undue emotionalism and all was impressive. This was the regular pattern from most of the meetings for several weeks with undiminished audiences and widespread interest. Billy Graham himself was a splendid figure, tall, erect, and earnest. He spoke invariably with an open Bible in his hand, and with an air of authority which complete conviction can give. The songs and choruses were triumphant and appealing.

For the closing rally of the Crusade, Hampden Park Football Ground was engaged. It was an unforgettable sight, the stands and terracing filled by a vast assembly of a hundred thousand people. After the usual singing of choruses, conducted by Cliff Barrows, and solos by Donald O'Shea, Billy Graham spoke for about half an hour on "Choose this day whom you will serve", and then appealed to people to come forward and make a decision for Christ. Two thousand three hundred came, standing in a huge circle round the grass pitch; the whole audience sitting in absolute silence and reverence as dusk filled the sky; a memorable end to a memorable mission. In the following months there was discussion on the methods and results of the Crusade. I think it is probably true that not many complete outsiders were drawn into the Christian community through the meetings, but the faith of many church members was undoubtedly strengthened and deepened. The Crusade enjoyed great publicity in the press, and at least for those weeks religion became a talking point in many unexpected places up and down the country. No mean achievement!

My wife and I came to know Billy Graham well, and I had many interesting and intimate talks with him. He is a man conscious of a divine call, and attributes all the amazing success of his missions to the power of God and of prayer, his own prayers and the prayers of his many supporters in many lands. Some years after the Scottish campaign, I found myself in New York when he was conducting a crusade in Madison Square Garden. He invited me to sit with him on the platform, from which one looked down across a vast audience of nineteen thousand. The hall had been filled with that number every evening for two months. The speaking was as trenchant, as serious, as moving as ever. One could not help rejoicing that at the very heart of that strange huge city where so many voices competed for attention, the Christian Good News was being sounded out with such power and conviction.

In 1952 the whole country was saddened by the death of the King, a man of simple tastes and high ideals, of courage and compassion. He and the Queen had stayed in London throughout the whole course of the war, sharing the dangers of their people. At the service of thanksgiving for his life the Cathedral was crowded to the doors by a congregation drawn from every section.

Next year at the coronation of the young Queen Elizabeth, Professor John Baillie and I, senior Royal Chaplains in Scotland, were commanded to walk in the Queen's procession. The occasion was memorable and magnificent beyond all words; the nave of the Abbey was transformed by the installation of high tiers of seats, filled by worshippers representative of every aspect of the life of the nation; the high altar glittering with silver and gold communion plate; the music superbly exultant; the complicated and moving ceremonial all rehearsed and carried out under the faultless direction of the Earl Marshal, the late Duke of Norfolk. The chief liturgical part of the service and the act of coronation were conducted by Geoffrey Fisher, Archbishop of Canterbury, with a combination of formality and simplicity, and the Queen herself, for whom the service must have been a testing ordeal, displayed serenity and dignity from beginning to end.

I found myself sitting next to that veteran warrior, the Reverend "Tubby" Clayton. After about an hour he became faint, and a member of St John's Ambulance Brigade tried to persuade him to leave the Church. In spite of her efforts, nothing would induce him to do so. Instead he sat for about half an hour with his head bent between his legs, after which he revived and stayed until the end of the service. How triumphantly have the hopes of that day been fulfilled. It has not been an easy period, but amid all the Queen has retained trust and respect for the monarchy. And at her side has stood her husband, Prince Philip.

In 1955 I was faced with a difficult decision. Dr Charles Warr announced that after his long ministry in St Giles he would like the presbytery to approve the appointment of a colleague to share the ministry with him and to succeed him. To my surprise I received a letter from one of the leading members of the kirk session to ask if I would allow my name to be proposed. If so, he had good reason to think it would be unanimously accepted. After a few days of consideration and discussion with my wife, I became convinced that I ought not to leave Glasgow. I had not yet seen the completion of our scheme for glass and furnishing in the Cathedral. Most difficult of all would have been to explain to my own beloved people in Glasgow why I should move at that stage in my life. For these and other reasons, I wrote a grateful but negative reply to my friend in Edinburgh.

Another outstanding event was an invitation for us to spend a fortnight in Germany as guests of the German government. On its practical side the visit was remarkably care-free because at every town visited we were met by a representative of the German International Department and taken care of day by day. The beginning was slightly inauspicious. We had travelled by air to Hamburg, only to discover on arrival that all our luggage was missing. Our host announced that a small reception had been arranged for me to meet leading ecclesiastics of all the churches in the city, and would take place almost at once. I had travelled in the most casual clothes, but there was nothing to be done. A few minutes later I had to walk into the reception room in old grey flannel trousers and tweed coat, to be greeted by an assembly of clergy, bishops, and pastors, all garbed in traditional black frock coats. My apologies were soon made, and I was welcomed. My wife meanwhile had been promised that if our luggage had not been recovered by the following day, she would be taken to the shops and invited to choose a whole new outfit. She was rather disappointed when the luggage arrived late that evening.

The German authorities had written to ask if there were any special aspects of the country I would like to see. I replied that I should be interested to see new churches built since the war and also art galleries. Our request was generously fulfilled. On our first day in Hamburg we were taken to see four new churches, of very modern design, in the suburbs of Hamm and Horn, and the new and impressive St Nicolai Church, built to replace the mediaeval city church, which had been almost completely destroyed. On the same day one of the leading churchmen, Hauptpastor Harms, showed us round his enormous church, St Michael's, with its majestic pulpit and altar and three organs. In the evening our escort took us to the opera and then supper in a nearby restaurant.

From Hamburg we went to Hanover, Dusseldorf, Munich, and the beautiful mountain country round Oberammergau and Garmisch, with its simple village churches and, at the opposite extreme, the superb baroque churches of Wies, Ettal, and Polling. I talked with leading churchmen like Preses Beckmann and Superintendent Stofer. The churches in Germany faced much the same problems as ourselves, including a diminishing number of men for the ministry. Germany had suffered much greater devastation in its cities and, perhaps for that reason, it seemed that they were more ready for changes and experiments in church life and evangelism. Many new churches symbolized new liturgical insights, the altar being frequently set almost at the centre of the church. New Roman Catholic churches were astonishingly simple and austere with almost no statues or pictures. More than once my wife asked me if we were in a Lutheran or Roman Catholic Church.

It seemed that there was a remarkable alertness to the opportunities of a strange and new religious situation. I was greatly impressed by the Evangelical Academies. We were taken to visit two. One at Loccum, in quiet country about twenty miles from Hanover was run by its Director, Dr Bolinsky, and his wife, a psychiatrist. The house accommodated a hundred and thirty and was splendidly equipped with a good staff and several lecture and reading rooms. The other was at the village of Tutzing in an old castle on the edge of Starnberger See. These provided courses on a wide range of subjects, social, artistic, cultural, and religious, and were planned for men and women "in the world." There was a mid-day act of intercession in the chapel, but the whole atmosphere was in no sense narrowly religious but calculated to encourage a wide view of the world and to make it possible for people to discover their priorities.

After some days at Munich we were taken to West Berlin and committed to the care of Frau Erna Colvenbach, a charming guide. We were driven round all the centre of the city to see splendidly restored buildings and older churches. Everywhere one got the impression of vitality. The only tragic feature was that every now and again one was confronted by the Wall, bleak, hostile, wicked in appearance, with desolate abandoned buildings all round, and East Berlin guards on duty everywhere. On one day we were escorted by a young Lebanese student to "Check-point Charlie" where, after showing passports, we were allowed to pass through and enter East Berlin. Things have improved since 1964 but my diary records, "A different world, with an atmosphere of sadness, suspicion and sordidness. Many of the finest buildings, churches, opera-house, palace, still in ruins, including the great Lutheran Cathedral. The beautiful mediaeval Church of St Mary fortunately undamaged and still in use. Comparatively few cars in the streets, pathetically dull and cheap looking shops, and no one smiling or cheerful. We drove along one magnificent new street, the Karl Marx Allee, with rows of flats and new public buildings. But everywhere dreariness and desolation." Frau Colvenbach's old mother lived just on the eastern side of the Wall. One could see the windows of her flat from the street in West Berlin. But only once in the year, at Christmas, was Frau Colvenbach allowed to cross to visit her mother.

We were taken to visit that great indomitable churchman, Bishop Dibelius, at his house in Dahlem. Owing to his courageous Christian utterances he was forbidden to visit the eastern half of his diocese, but contrived to keep in close touch with it. He told us of the practical difficulties put in the way of church projects. The Communist government professed to allow complete religious freedom but if, for example, it was proposed to build a new church, they would be told that no bricks were available. If a well-wisher offered to provide the bricks, it would be said that no labour could be spared. When a congregation announced arrangements for Sunday School and youth activities they would be informed that the civic authorities expected all young people to attend officially arranged secular programmes. Despite frustrations the great old leader, then in his eightyfifth year, was confident that nothing would extinguish the faith of his people and that persecution might even deepen it.

I also had long conversations with Lutheran clergy, among them Pastor von der Hude and Pastor Cavar, about new modes of worship and pastoral care. Berlin, like most large cities, holds many suffering from nervous strain. In such cases even a talk with a sympathetic listener can save a person from a nervous breakdown and possible suicide. In the church built around the ruins of the huge Kaiser Wilhelm Memorial Church, there were small rooms for the different clergy, each with his name on the door. All round the clock it is open with at least one pastor on duty so that a person in trouble may find someone to give sympathy and help. We came home touched by the kindness and courtesy shown us and with new ideas.

The highlight of that year, both for the Cathedral congregation and myself, was a visit from the Queen. She had no other official engagements and simply wanted to attend our ordinary morning service. The date was 28 June, and a few days before it I had a message from Buckingham Palace that Her Majesty did not want me to confine myself to the proposed list of people to be presented, but to feel free to present anyone I wished. She would sit for the first time in the Royal pew which we had installed some time previously. The great day came and the Cathedral, both nave and choir, was filled from end to end. I had invited Dr Charles Warr of St Giles and Dr John Lamb of Crathie to take part. I preached on Deuteronomy XI v.11,"a land of hills and valleys." The choir sang an anthem specially composed by our Master of the Music, Wilfred Emery, "Allelujah, Honour, and Praise be to God." Among the hymns. I had chosen one of my favourites, "Summer suns are glowing". Faith was justified and brilliant sunlight streamed into the church from beginning to end. Afterwards I was able to show the Queen the Blacader Aisle, the lower church, and the shrine of St Mungo, and to present many members of our kirk session and congregation and not least George Mitchell, the senior beadle, who had been my constant helper for twentyfive years.

A wealthy and generous citizen of Glasgow had set up an unusual trust by which a gold medal and a gift of £1,000 was to be presented, once in three years, to the person who, in the opinion of a representative panel, "had done most in the previous three years to make Glasgow more beautiful, healthier, or more honoured." The chairman of the committee was the lord provost in office. Nominations were invited from societies, charities, and groups of all kinds. One winter afternoon, when I was laid up with a bout of bronchitis, the telephone rang. A few minutes later Flora, our housekeeper, came to my room with a puzzled look on her face. She said, "That was a message from the lord provost's secretary. He wanted to let you know that you had won some kind of prize; so that you might get the news before an announcement is made to the papers. I couldn't understand properly what he meant. And I think it may be some sort of hoax." When my wife came in shortly afterwards, the telephone rang again, and she discovered that I had been elected to receive the Saint Mungo Prize. It was duly presented at a ceremony in the City Chambers. It gave me particular pleasure as a mark of trust and affection from many representative people in the great city that I loved.

10

Moderatorial Year

Unlike the Church of England, which is governed by bishops, the Scottish Church is ordered by a graded series of courts, kirk session, presbytery, synod, and General Assembly. Each is presided over by a minister who is known as a moderator, and in the last three cases holds office for a year. In the case of the General Assembly the moderator is the chief representative of the Church on all kinds of occasions, and in Scotland, during his year of office, he takes official precedence after the royal dukes as the senior minister of the National Church. The Moderator is chosen by a committee consisting of the previous moderators and representatives from the synods. His main duties are to preside at meetings of the General Assembly and the Commission of Assembly, to pay official visits to some six or seven presbyteries, to visit units of the Armed Forces, and to represent his Church on ecumenical or public occasions. To make this possible he is set free for a year from his own parish duties. To this rather daunting responsibility I was called for the General Assembly of 1962.

In recognition of the National Church the Sovereign appoints a Lord High Commissioner to represent him or her, to bring a royal greeting, and to take back an official report. While the Assembly sits he resides in Holyroodhouse and entertains ministers, elders, and visitors from many walks of life. During sessions of the Assembly he sits in the throne gallery as an observer, but takes no part except for a short greeting at the opening and closing. There is nothing comparable to this elsewhere. It symbolises the relationship between Church and State in Scotland. In England the Sovereign is the head of the Church, and the Church is in important ways under the jurisdiction of Parliament, but the Scottish Church, though recognised as the National Church, has complete spiritual freedom in doctrine and worship, in administration and the choice of her clergy. The Sovereign's representative at the Assembly illustrates in a simple and dramatic way the place of the Church in the life of our nation. It was fortunate for me that in my year as moderator the Lord High Commissioner was the Earl of Mansfield, whose wife is a cousin of my own.

The first duty of the moderator is to preside at all the chief sessions during the ten days in the second fortnight of May when the Assembly meets. It is a large body of about fourteen hundred members, half of them ministers and half of them elders, representative of every presbytery and drawn from all parts from the Mull of Galloway to the Shetlands. Debates cover a wide range from ecclesiastical matters to social and moral welfare, conditions in agriculture and industry. There are always elders of specialised knowledge and experience whose guidance can be counted upon. Through its committees, working during the winter months, the Assembly provides much serious thinking and in its debates lively speaking on many topics. The press usually gives good reports and recommendations can be sent to government departments.

For the moderator it is an arduous experience. In addition to presiding he has to speak at large women's meetings, to attend social functions, and to give a closing address of substance. Every morning begins with devotions which he conducts. Sir Arthur Bryant, taken to the Assembly one day, said afterwards that he would never forget the unaccompanied singing of the psalm by fifteen hundred men's voices. My wife and I stayed during the Assembly at the Roxburghe Hotel where we had a pleasant sitting room and bedroom, looking out across the gardens to the Georgian houses of Charlotte Square. We also had rooms for my two chaplains, the Reverend W.H. Rogan of Paisley Abbey, and the Reverend Tom Kiltie of Whitehill, Stepps, and their wives. From time to time we had an hour to ourselves and occasionally one or two people to dinner. On Thursday evening we had the traditional Moderator's Reception in the Signet Library with four hundred guests.

There were many festivities at Holyrood. My wife and I were invited to stay for the weekend and found an interesting party of other guests, the Danish Ambassador, the High Commissioner for Australia, Sir Eric Harrison and his wife, Lord and Lady Hailsham, General Sir John and Lady Kennedy, Sir William Lithgow, the shipbuilder, and John Richardson. After a somewhat violent argument with Hailsham over the nuclear deterrent, he chaffed me gleefully over the eighteenth century moderatorial coat and breeches. On Sunday evening, after service and ceremonial, the atmosphere was relaxed. Sir Eric Harrison recited Australian ballads, Lord Glentanar sat down at the piano and sang Scottish songs, and one of the A.D.C.s did some conjuring tricks. On Wednesday evening, the Assembly closed with my address on "The Vocation of the Church" and all stood in silence while there were read out the names of ministers who in the last twelve months had passed on into fuller light.

The next major duty was the visitation of seven presbyteries and I decided to do this, if possible, before the end of the year. Some had been chosen because they had had no such visit for several years, and some for personal reasons. My presbyteries were Wigtown and Stranraer, Linlithgow and Falkirk, Mull, Meigle, Turriff, Deer, and Caithness.

About a fortnight was spent in each. The programme varied from one area to another, but included worship, conferences with ministers, receptions by the provost and magistrates of burghs, visits to secondary schools, industrial works, and hospitals. It gave a panoramic view of the contemporary Church in town and country, industrial towns and rural communities.

Particular events stand out in memory. I think of a service in the small parish church of Leswalt in Wigtownshire, built by my own great-grandfather as chief heritor almost exactly a hundred years previously. As I preached I could imagine him and his family sitting in the Agnew pew on Sunday mornings. In Caithness, by contrast, the presbytery clerk escorted us to the nuclear power station at Dounreay, with its two and a half thousand employees and scores of graduate scientists. We lunched with the controller, Dr Hirst, the deputy director, Mr Carmichael, and other senior executives. After putting on a helmet and special clothes, and being escorted through bolted doors, we entered the great steel sphere, with its incredibly complicated machinery, in which the uranium is processed. Here were men working with cosmic forces, which they themselves could not yet fully understand, and with immeasureable potentialities. As scientific knowledge and technical skill expand, how urgent is the need for matching wisdom and self discipline.

I completed the visitation before the end of the year. The warmth of the welcome made a strenuous duty also a delight. It was easy to draw optimistic conclusions about the state of the Church, but one had also to be realistic. Yet, looking back I feel that in all kinds of unexpected places many people hearing the great name of God, responded with at least a whispered affirmative. For about three months in the early part of 1963, my wife and I found ourselves travelling a good deal. I was asked to visit Scottish troops serving in the Middle East and in January we flew out to Aden, where the Scots Greys and the first Battalion of the King's Own Scottish Borderers were serving. From both units and from men serving with the Royal Air Force and the 45 Commando Royal Marines I received the kindest welcome and was glad to bring them greetings from the home Church. Stationed on the edge of the desert, the Scots Greys found it extremely difficult to keep their armoured vehicles in good order among the dust and sand storms.

We stayed for a fortnight with the Army Commander, Major-General James Robertson in his pleasant house high above the town. By constant watering he contrived to have his garden always green and full of flowers and it was often refreshed by small sea breezes. Seated beside the pilot I flew in a very small plane up into the hills at Dhala to visit troops of the Federal Army who had some British officers and N.C.O.s. They were stationed five thousand feet up and only a few miles from the Yemeni border where fighting was going on between royalists and republicans.

Them we went on over a mass of fantastically shaped rocky mountains to Makriras where there were more troops and where we lunched in the mess. I got the impression that in such remote surroundings the men felt they were on active service and were more contented than in Aden.

For long the Church of Scotland had a mission station at Sheik-Othman — a discouraging sphere of evangelism. Christian influence in a Muslim country makes little impact and conversions are few. One obstacle is that if a Muslim becomes a Christian it is almost impossible for him to find a woman prepared to marry him so that he has no prospect of a happy family life. But the hospital and the youth club rooms were greatly appreciated and our missionaries, the Reverend James Ritchie, Miss Cowie, and Dr Robertson, were people of immense faith and courage. Since then our mission has had to be brought to an end and the work left in the hands of Arab Christians.

From Aden we flew to Nairobi, where we were guests of the Deputy Assistant Chaplain-General, Canon John Brown, and his wife. There we met an old lady who told us how she first came from the coast to Nairobi fifty years before in a convoy of horse drawn wagons. It consisted of a general store and a few roughly constructed houses and huts, but today it is a large prosperous modern town of wide handsome streets lined with trees and flowering shrubs, imposing new buildings of all kinds, even a theatre. At least in technical and commercial terms civilization moves fast in modern Africa. I was able to visit the second Battalion of the Scots Guards at Kahala and drive to the big R.A.F. station at Eastleigh. Sunday was spent at the beautiful outlying station of Gilgil with Colonel Charles Napier and the Gordon Highlanders. After early communion we had a service in the little Church of Goodwill built by Lady Eleanor Cole as a thanksgiving that her two sons had come safely through the war. Soldiers, farmers and coffee planters filled the building and the singing was splendid.

These names and events belong to a chapter in British history that is closed, and British troops will no longer be called to serve in that wonderful country. Independence for Kenya was near. Malcolm Macdonald, the last governor, had just taken up his post, a man with a gift of understanding different races. We were invited to lunch with him and his Canadian wife. He had only arrived some ten days previously, and one of his staff told me that he worked almost round the clock, spending all day in meeting key people and half the night in reading reports and documents concerned with the recent history of Kenya, to prepare the country for independence.

Apart from many functions we had two memorable experiences. One was a long drive into a game park where we saw in their natural surroundings giraffe, zebra, wild pigs, wildebeeste, gazelle, and a family of lion cubs at play. As for the other, Air Commodore Macdonald, affectionately known as "Black Mac", insisted that we must make an expedition up country. When I told him that we had hardly a spare moment he said, "Would you mind getting up really early one morning? I still keep a very small plane at my disposal, which I fly myself. If you and your wife would care, I would fly you round Mount Kenya as the sun is rising; a rather magnificent sight, and on the way back you would get a panoramic view of the countryside." We got up at 6.30 a.m., drove out to the airport, and he took us up in a small plane piloted by himself. I sat beside him in the co-pilot's seat. We flew northwards over the coffee plantations, the African reserve, the rich farm land of the Rift Valley, and round the snow streaked rocky summit of Mount Kenya, superb in the clear light of early morning.

Crowded days in Nairobi passed all too quickly. We had been invited by the Reverend John Fleming, Director of the Colleges in South-East Asia, to spend a long weekend in Singapore. We stayed with him and his wife at the United Theological College to meet students of many races preparing for the Christian ministry. On Sunday morning I preached in St Andrew's Presbyterian Church for a service broadcast throughout Malaya and in the evening in the Anglican Cathedral. The church was crowded and the atmosphere humid; I was wearing heavy robes and never felt so hot in any pulpit. Afterwards we recovered when Bishop Kenneth Sansbury took us to a small dinner party in the Raffles Hotel. Little did I think at the time that in a few years I should enjoy his friendship when he became secretary of the British Council of Churches. Next day John Fleming gave a tea party in the College where we met about eighty representatives of all the churches in Singapore, and in the evening Lord Selkirk, the High Commissioner for South East Asia, gave a reception in our honour at which we shook hands with a long procession. We left Singapore wondering how people from the west can live an active life and remain alert in such a climate.

Some months previously I had been asked to spend February in Melbourne where the Scots Church was celebrating its one hundred and twentyfifth anniversary as a congregation. From Singapore we flew to Darwin. Our plane touched down in the middle of the night, but even at that time the temperature was in the eighties. We managed to get a room in the primitive but expensive hotel. The room had eight beds in it! Next morning after some hours of sleep we walked round the town, with its broad streets and simple buildings, many on stilts. Farmers and cattlemen from scattered stations and remote homesteads met here and aborigines, fine upstanding men, mixed easily with other races in this cosmopolitan town. Only gradually can a people whose roots go back into the Stone Age be integrated into the sophisticated society of the white races. They have their own myths and traditions, their own art, nomadic ways, separate tribes and customs. Great stretches of country, especially in the north, have been reserved for these people to live their own life and practise their own customs. Missions work among them. The minister of the Australian Presbyterian Church in Darwin, the Reverend Ronald Thomas, drove us round the town and into open country. Wallabies were grazing and loping about among the eucalyptus trees. Our destination was a Roman Catholic hospital run by nuns for aborigines with leprosy. There was a remarkably happy atmosphere due to the faith and dedication of the sisters, women who had left friends and families and civilized life to live in a remote region and a trying climate to care for the suffering of one of the most primitive races in the world.

After two days we went on by air to Melbourne. Our visit was partly under the auspices of the Turnbull Trust and we were welcomed on arrival by the minister of the Scots Church, the Reverend A. Crichton Barr, the session clerk, and several members of the Trust. On Sunday Crichton Barr drove us to the Scots Church, a handsome building on a magnificent site. The congregation filled the church which seated a thousand people and included the Governor, General Sir Dallas Brooks and his wife, the Honourable A.J. Fraser representing the Premier, and the Moderator of the Church in Victoria, the Right Reverend J.P. Chalinor and his wife. I preached on "The Christian Foundations of Society" and the lessons were read by the Moderator and the Governor. On 24 February the Queen and Prince Philip attended a service of commemoration. Prince Philip read the lesson, Crichton Barr preached, and at the close the Queen unveiled and I dedicated a stained glass window.

Thanks to the kindness of many we had long drives in the country, to the Yanyean reservoir with its thousands of acres of grassland and troops of kangaroos, to the Healesville Sanctuary with its parrots of many colours, lyre-birds, bower birds, and koala bears, to the immense stretch of Eildon Water, and to old homesteads and estates. A kinsman of mine, Lord de L'Isle, was Governor General at the time, and we spent two days with him in Government House and had a glimpse of Canberra, a city of officials. My wife had cousins, Bill and Molly Lyon, in the western district of Victoria, and we spent some days at their sheep station at Wonominta, "the watering place of the kangaroo and the emu." One morning I addressed a thousand senior boys at the great Presbyterian school, Scotch College. Another day at Haileybury School, where Mr Menzies, the Prime Minister, had two grandsons, he declared the new buildings open and I said the prayer of dedication. All was done in the open air.

Our friend, Sir Bernard Fergusson, the Governor General of New Zealand, invited us to Government House in Auckland before returning to Scotland and when he made our coming known the church authorities sent me a request for a programme of three weeks. At Government House we met many figures in New Zealand life, notably the ex-Premier,

Mr Nash, then 81 but extremely alert in mind. Bernard Fergusson was a popular Governor. His father had once held the same position and his mother had given him as a boy of fourteen a New Testament in the Maori language. When he returned as Governor he renewed his knowledge of the language to address Maori audiences in their own tongue. After visiting a cousin and her husband, Dr Rufus Rodger, now a member of the New Zealand Parliament, I fulfilled a round of preaching engagements in Hamilton, Auckland, Wellington, Christchurch, and Dunedin. In Dunedin especially the Scottish tradition is still strong. There, after many years, I met the Reverend Dr John Allan, Principal of Knox College, the most brilliant student of theology in New College, Edinburgh, in the nineteen twenties. Everywhere one was conscious of how greatly the people of New Zealand, at the other end of the world, still cherish the ways which their forebears carried from Britain.

Almost exactly half way round the globe, we decided to return by the United States, flying from Auckland with short stops at Fiji and Honolulu. At Los Angeles we stayed with an old friend, the Reverend Dr Geddes McGregor, Dean of the Faculty of Religion at the University of Southern California. He showed us round the spacious campus, the sumptuous residences of film stars, and the fabulous cemetery, Forest Lawn, where the associations of death are disguised under crude sentimentality and extravagance. From Los Angeles we flew to San Francisco, surely one of the most beautiful cities of the world above its wide Bay. For two days we stayed in Grace Cathedral Church House by invitation of that brilliant but erratic ecclesiastic, the late Bishop James Pike; a man who had turned from his early agnosticism to the Christian faith and had then passed through a whole gamut of churchmanship, Presbyterian, Roman Catholic, and finally Anglican. A forceful personality, he was one of the outstanding figures in the religious scene at that time. Ecumenically minded, he welcomed people of all Christian traditions to his Cathedral.

From San Francisco we flew three thousand miles across the States in five hours. In New York snow was lying in the streets and winter was still in the air. After a few days with our friends, Lawrence and Jessie Gaylord in New Jersey, we set off on our last stage, reaching Scotland in early spring. We had been away for three months.

11

Retirement

After reaching sixtyfive and having spent some thirty years in a very demanding sphere I thought of finding a quiet country parish where I could still give some years of service, but leading members of the kirk session discussed it frankly with me and I was persuaded to remain. After two or three years I became convinced that the hour had come. Change was everywhere in the air. Long accepted moral standards and religious traditions were being questioned and even the face of Glasgow was undergoing drastic change. A new voice was needed in the pulpit of the mother church of the city, and a different mind to grapple with new problems. On a Sunday in the autumn of 1966 I informed the congregation that I intended to retire in the following spring. Emotionally it was the most difficult announcement I have ever had to make, for the pastoral relationship, especially if it is a long one, is strong and deep. My wife and I knew many families intimately. I had shared their joys and their griefs and anxieties. I had sat with them in their homes, talking of many things. I had spoken to them on Sundays from the pulpit, praying that my words might be "in the Name of the Father, and of the Son, and of the Holy Spirit." I had shared with them the sacrament at the Lord's Table. I had baptised their children, officiated at the marriage of their sons and daughters and at the final committal of loved ones into the safe keeping of God. It is not easy to break such associations.

Glasgow must be one of the friendliest cities in the country; its people are warm hearted and outgoing. Of course, like all big cities, it has its rough and unruly elements. There is far too much juvenile delinquency — to use the modern jargon — and much of it is due to a lack of open spaces and recreational facilities. It has a good deal of violent behaviour. In the unfashionable street where my wife and I lived for more than twenty years three murders took place at different times, and for some years there was a police patrol during the night in winter. On the other hand there was a friendly kind of community feeling, and I usually said, "Good morning", even to strangers whom I met on our hill, as naturally as if it had been a country village street. Among our neighbours were Indians, Cypriots, Maltese, and Italians. Glasgow absorbs other nationalities without resentment. It was amusing to hear a small Pakistani boy suddenly break into a flow of speech in the broadest Glasgow accent. I can never be grateful enough that so many years were spent in that great noisy, busy, vigorous, kind-hearted city, and in that splendid mediaeval church where for more than seven hundred years prayer and worship have continued.

I chose Easter Sunday as the last day of my ministry there. The beloved Cathedral was filled with a large congregation. The music was superb. There was a wonderful sense of reverence and fellowship. Even through my personal sorrow of farewell, I was conscious of the transcendent joy of the Easter triumph. Then, for my wife and myself, there were hundreds of loving hand-shakes and kind wishes for the future.

A minister of religion is in a peculiarly happy position. Ordination is to a lifelong vocation, and a man never really retires from the ordained ministry. He is able to give his help in preaching, the sacraments, and pastoral care. This is a great consolation and means that his later years need hardly ever feel dull or useless. Feeling that it was wiser to leave Glasgow and begin a new chapter, my wife and I had to decide where to make our home. Our choice was limited. My wife's mother was now in Haddington; I was a member of several Assembly committees; and we felt it better to be in reach of a town. So we decided to find a house in East Lothian, Fife, or Berwickshire.

In our minds we had a picture of the house we hoped to find: small, yet large enough for visitors and with space for books, built of stone in Scottish style, and if possible in the eighteenth or early nineteenth century, and, of course, at a reasonable price. Finally, I saw in *The Scotsman* one morning the advertisement of a house exactly what we were searching for. It was in the village of West Barns, two miles from Dunbar, in East Lothian. That afternoon we drove to see it and found it all we had hoped for, and bought it that same evening. Dating from the middle of the eighteenth century, it is of the plainest design but strongly built, harled and whitewashed. It stands on the bank of a tiny river, the Biel Water, on a private road leading only to a ford. To the east it is sheltered by high trees, and the west looks across farm land to the Bass Rock, North Berwick Law, and Traprain Law. There is a small but interesting garden, an old pantiled garden shed and garage and the little domain is surrounded by an eight-foot wall of local red sandstone. It has a dining room, a small study, a pleasant upstairs drawingroom, a bedroom and dressing room for my wife and myself, and another for friends. Here we moved from Glasgow.

Outsiders often associate East Lothian with the rather sophisticated communities of North Berwick, Gullane, and Dunbar; but all over the county are unspoilt villages such as Athelstaneford and Stenton where life goes on at a leisurely tempo. Retirement had advantages; one no longer lived under the tyranny of the clock. In Glasgow the weeks had seemed too short and the days impossibly full. One's conscience was continually troubled. Sermons and speeches had to be too hurriedly prepared. Pastoral visitation was curtailed. There was too little time for prayer and meditation. And the pace of life in a large city creates mental and moral strain. For forty years I had lived an intensely active life and I dreaded the possibility of unwanted idleness. But if you decide to live in the country gradually you discover the countryman's superior art of living; to each day what has to be done, but to do it without haste or anxiety. Country life is more sane and healthy. Assembly committees still took me to Edinburgh two or three times a week. A vacancy occurred in the large parish of St Mary's, Haddington; the presbytery asked me to act as interim moderator in the vacancy, and I was able to help them choose a young and vigorous minister, the Reverend James Riach. With my new freedom I was able to accept requests to preach at special occasions of all kinds such as Holy Week services or the leading of a retreat for clergy.

Since the second world war vast changes have taken place in the pattern of social life and religious outlook. Realising this the General Assembly of 1967 set up a special committee to consider the "Training and Recruitment for the Ministry." I was appointed convener, and for two years it occupied much of my time and thought. It was necessary to visit all four theological faculties and colleges in St Andrews, Edinburgh, Glasgow, and Aberdeen and to have conference with staff and students. In Scotland training for the ministry is undertaken, not in independent colleges as in England, but in close association with the four older universities. Theological professors are appointed by a joint board and so long as this close and understanding relationship can be maintained the Church benefits greatly. By an excellent tradition the Scottish Church has demanded a high standard of education which usually meant six or seven years of study. In recent years this has been relaxed. There are men without great intellectual ability who have other gifts and a great contribution to make. For this reason the Committee made a strong plea for a wide and imaginative variety of courses. This recommendation was approved. It was also recommended that there should be closer communication between the faculties so that divinity students would avoid the temptation to think of theology in isolation from other fields. A strong plea was also made for more specialist ministries. Never have there been such frontier situations for theology. The Church has no residential college. More opportunities for worship and prayer were required. It was therefore recommended that students should have the experience of living and worshipping as a community for some time. Unfortunately this has been carried no further. It did, however, inspire the Assembly to hold In Service Courses for ministers.

In 1974 the small Waldensian Evangelical Church in Italy celebrated its eighth centenary and I gladly represented the Church of Scotland. High up in the wild mountain country between Turin and the French frontier lives the Waldenses whose survival through eight hundred years is a remarkable phenomenon. They have never been numerous and at times have been subject to cruel persecution. Tracing their origin to Waldo, a merchant of Lyons in the twelfth century, they have consistently stood for certain convictions, a deep love of the Bible, a passionate belief in religious freedom, and a cultivation of simplicity both in worship and in way of life. In 1184 the Council of Verona excommunicated them. In the fourteenth century they united with the movement of John Hus to form what has been called "the First Reformation", and in 1532 at the Synod of Chamforam they officially took their place in the family of Reformed Churches. Fierce repression took place in the sixteenth century when those living in Provence, Calabria, and Piedmont were massacred without mercy. Many fled to Germany and Switzerland but a few thousand dared to remain in the valleys of the Pellice and Chisone region. Further attempts to exterminate them followed, but in spite of all they survived. Only in 1848 did this change when an edict gave them civil rights and allowed them to organise as a recognised Christian community. The annual meeting of their synod, usually at Torre Pellice, is presided over by a moderator. Their numbers are small; thirty thousand in Italy and Sicily, with about eighty churches and a hundred ministers and evangelists, and some sixteen thousand whose forebears emigrated to Uruguay. Today there is still a strong recognition of doctrinal differences, but friendliness and tolerance make mutual respect possible. The Reverend Malcolm Ritchie and I attended the synod to bring greetings and congratulations, and received the kindest possible welcome. As we visited their remote valleys we were reminded of our own Covenanters. Perhaps the most significant building we were shown was the Agape Youth Ecumenical Centre.

As I write, another winter and spring have gone by, and the garden is full of sunshine and flowers. A pair of spotted fly-catchers laid four delicately marked eggs in a crevice in the wall by the garden gate. The young have now hatched and the parents are busy feeding them. When not taking food to the nest, one or other takes station on a laburnum close by and talks for minutes on end to the young ones. Looking back across the years of the century through which I have lived, the chief impression is that of change, especially social and economic. We have a more just and well balanced pattern of national life, and yet there are other less happy features. I think if I were not a Christian I would be a pessimist but, being a Christian, I cannot. Beneath all the cruelty and greed and hatred the ever-living Christ is still at work, striving by His Spirit to change the hearts and minds of men and women. There is a great divine purpose of love running through the whole chequered process of history and in the end that purpose will prevail.

My last word must be one of thankfulness. As I look back I see myself continually surrounded by blessings beyond calculation, a vocation full of interest and reward, a marriage of perfect happiness, a wonderfully wide circle of friends, the unfailing companionship of books, some old and familiar, some new and exciting, and the endlessly varied beauties of this earth, skyscape and landscape, trees, flowers, and birds, especially birds. And over-arching all the years there is the unfailing providence and kindness of God, the great Father and King, to Whom be praise and thanksgiving.